This book is to be returned on or before
the last date stamped

HOLT LIBRARY
(01263) 712202

21. FEB 06.
21. NOV 05.

23 MAY 06

*Gatehouse at Bungay*

# THE CASTLES
# OF EAST ANGLIA

## Mike Salter

FOLLY PUBLICATIONS

# ACKNOWLEDGEMENTS

The photographs in this book were mostly taken by the author in 1999-2000, although a number of old postcards from his collection have also been reproduced. The author also drew the plans and the map. Plans are mostly drawn to common scales of 1:400 for keeps and gatehouses, 1:800 for courtyard buildings, and 1:2000 and 1:4000 for site plans of earthworks. Thanks to Lorna Harrison for help with accommodation and transport during work in Essex in 1999.

## AUTHOR'S NOTES

This series of books (see full list inside back cover) are intended as portable field guides giving as much information and illustrative material as possible in volumes of modest size, weight and price. As a whole the series gives a lot of information on lesser known sites about which little information has tended to appear in print. The aim in the castle books has been to mention, where the information is known to the author, owners or custodians of buildings who erecred or altered parts of them, and those who were the first or last to hold an estate, an inportant office, or a title. Those in occupation at the time of dramatic events such as sieges are also often named. Other owners and occupants whose lives had little effct on the condition of the buildings are generally not mentioned, nor are most 19th or 20th century events, ghost stories, or legends.

The books are intended to be used in conjunction with the Ordnance Survey 1:50,000 maps. Grid references are given in the gazetteers together with a coding system indicating which buildings can be visited or easily seen by the public which is explained on page 13. Generally speaking, maps will be required to find most of the lesser known earthworks, the majority of which are not regularly open to the public.

Each level of a building is called a storey in this book, the basement being the first or lowest storey with its floor near courtyard level unless mentioned as otherwise.

Measurements given in the text and scales on the plans are in metres, the unit used by the author for all measurements taken on site. Although the buildings were design using feet the metric scales are much easier to use and are now standard amongst those studying historicf buildings and ancient sites. For those who feel a need to make a conversion 3 metres is almost 10 feet. Unless specifically mentioned as otherwise all dimensions are external at or near ground level, but above the plinth if there is one. On plans the original work is shown black, post-1800 is stippled and alterations and additions of intermediate periods are hatched.

## ABOUT THE AUTHOR

Mike Salter is 47 and has been a professional writer and publisher since he went on the Government Enterprise Allowance Scheme for unemployed people in 1988. He is particularly interested in the planning and layout of medieval buildings and has a huge collection of plans of churches and castles he has measured during tours (mostly by bicycle and motorcycle) throughout all parts of the British Isles since 1968. Wolverhampton born and bred, Mike now lives in an old cottage beside the Malvern Hills. His other interests include walking, maps, railways, board games, morris dancing, playing percussion instruments and calling dances with a folk group.

First published February 2001. Copyright Mike Salter.
Folly Publications, Folly Cottage, 151 West Malvern Rd, Malvern, Worcs WR14 4AY
Printed by Aspect Design, 89 Newtown Rd, Malvern, Worcs WR14 2PD

L728-81

NORFOLK LIBRARY AND
INFORMATION SERVICE

| SUPP | CYP |
|---|---|
| INV.NO. | 867820 |
| ORD DATE | 1-9.03 |

*The keep at Castle Rising*

# CONTENTS

A map of buildings described appears inside the front cover

# INTRODUCTION

The type of defensible residence known to the Normans as a castle was introduced to England in the mid 11th century. There were Normans in England before Duke William of Normandy's successful invasion in 1066, but it was only then that they took control of the country. Having taken the English crown William granted estates to his followers in return for periods of military service. The Norman lords or barons then in turn gave units of land called manors to their knights, again in return for military service, this system being known as feudalism. The thin veneer of land-owning Normans consolidated their fragile hold on the land by constructing castles serving as residences, strongholds and as symbols of lordly rank. The Romans and Saxons built purely military forts and defences around settlements but the Normans introduced the idea of powerful individuals erecting fortresses to serve as their residences and as the administrative centres of groups of manors. The Domesday Book survey commissioned by William I in 1086 to record who was holding what land and what it was then considered to be worth, records quite a number of castles in East Anglia. These castles were generally not of mortared stone but of earth and wood, materials which allowed a more rapid construction and some prefabrication.

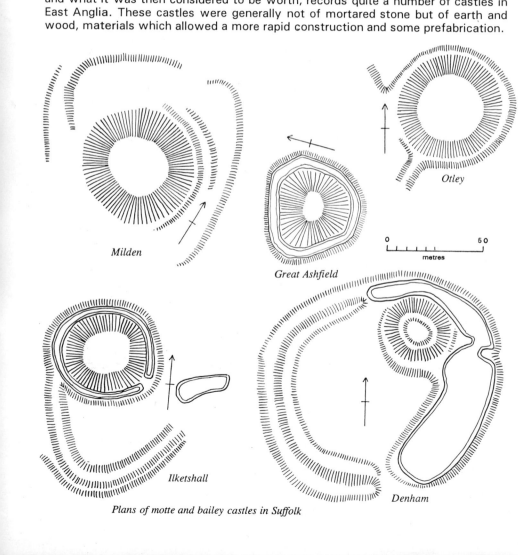

*Milden*

*Great Ashfield*

*Otley*

*Ilketshall*

*Denham*

0             5 0
metres

*Plans of motte and bailey castles in Suffolk*

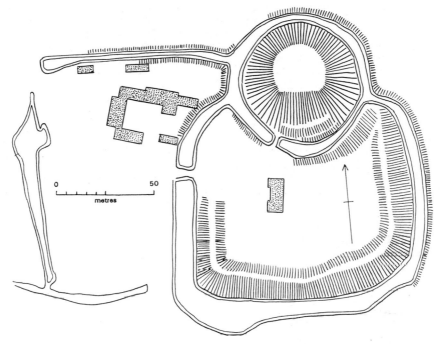

*Plan of Haughley Castle*

Castles built in the late 11th century often had a high mound raised from material taken out of the surrounding ditch and having on top the lord's residence in the form of a two or three storey timber tower surrounded by a palisade. The mound summit was reached by a ramp up from a forecourt or bailey in which were sited a range of stores, workshops, a hall and other apartments, and a chapel, all originally built of wood. Sometimes the mound took an alternative form called a ringwork with a high rampart surrounding the lord's house, and the greater castles usually had an additional outer bailey beyond the main entrance. Castles of these types continued to be built for over a century after the Norman Conquest and can only be precisely dated when there is a historical record of their foundation or good archaeological evidence, both of which are lacking for many of the sites described in this book. The castles of East Anglia are noted for their impressive earthworks, which in many cases outlived the stone walls and buildings later erected upon them. King William himself is thought to have erected the castles at Cambridge, Ely, Huntingdon, Norwich and possibly Thetford, all of which have or had large mounds. The mound at Norwich is mostly natural but the others are mostly artificial. Other fine motte and bailey castles in East Anglia include Clare, Great Canfield, Haughley, Ongar, Pleshey and Rayleigh. The massive earthworks at Castle Acre are now thought to be of the 1130s and 40s, whilst those at Castle Rising and New Buckenham seem to be mostly the product of refortification of those castles during the civil war of 1214-17. The most impressive castles tended to be the headquarters of great lords, whilst there were many smaller castles, built by their knights, who owed annual military service at the greater castles, this being the way feudalism worked.

*Middleton Motte*

For the first two generations after Duke William's invasion of 1066 masons were in short supply compared with carpenters and labourers, partly because the Saxons and Danes mostly erected buildings of wood except for the most important churches. Buildings of mortared stone took several years of comparatively peaceful conditions to construct. Fortifications would have been vulnerable to attack during the often quite long periods when foundations were being laid, so structures raised quickly on timber posts were seen as an easier option when defences were required in a hurry. Timber eventually rots when in contact with damp earth so when more peaceful conditions allowed wooden structures were gradually replaced by buildings of stone. Two buildings, however, were of stone from the start, although they were surrounded by earth ramparts and timber palisades. These are William I's keep at Colchester and the de Warennes' house at Castle Acre. Both contained a hall and private chamber side by side over dark basement rooms probably used for storage. The Colchester keep is the largest in Europe and seems to have been built in two stages. It is possible that the upper storey, although part of the original design, was not built until the beginning of the 12th century. The Colchester keep was a massively walled building, whilst the house at Castle Acre had walls less than half as thick and was probably not embattled in its original form. In the early 12th century Henry I built a keep at Norwich with the same basic plan as that at Colchester, but with a elaborately decorated outer shell. Both keeps have a chapel in the layout of the upper rooms, but whilst at Colchester there is a projecting apse to contain the chapel east end, at Norwich there is a just a tiny alcove within one corner of the building. In c1140 the Albini family built a keep at Castle Rising with a strikingly similar plan as that at Norwich, both of them having a kitchen tucked into the NW corner and being entered at the NE corner through a porch or fore-building reached by steps.

*Ringwork at Wormgay*

Also dating from the 1140s are two East Anglian keeps which are very different from each other. New Buckenham, another Albini fortress, has the lowest storey of a circular keep, larger than and at least half a century earlier than, any other keep of this type elsewhere in Britain. The de Vere Earl of Oxford's seat at Castle Hedingham has a square keep, but unlike Colchester, Norwich and Rising, it is a true tower, considerably taller than it is long or wide, and the cross-wall does not divide the upper rooms, for it there takes the form of an arch. It seems that this building, whilst an impregnable citadel and a symbol of lordship visible for miles around, was not a residence. It contains no sleeping spaces, chapel or kitchen, just a reception room over a basement and a court room above. The defaced lower parts remain of similar buildings, possibly of the 1140s but maybe of later in the 12th century, at Bungay, Mileham and Saffron Walden, the first two being on large but low mottes. Bungay belonged to Hugh Bigod, created Earl of Norfolk by King Stephen, during whose reign the East Anglian castles saw considerable action. Stephen himself besieged several of the castles, and in 1143 built several castles to contain the activities of Geoffrey de Mandeville, newly created Earl of Essex. Excavations at one of them, Burwell, where de Mandeville sustained his mortal wound whilst attacking the incomplete castle, revealed part of a curtain wall and gatehouse on a platform surrounded by a wide wet moat. A unusually high proportion of castles in East Anglia have water-filled moats, the general flatness of the land making this both possible and desirable, militarily speaking. Weeting has remains of a 12th century block containing a hall and chamber lying in the middle of a moated platform with no trace of any curtain wall. Castle Rising also has a rectangular gatehouse of c1140, whilst Castle Acre has one of c1120, and three others (including the town gate) of c1190.

After the chaos of civil war during King Stephen's reign (1135-54) the Crown attempted to exercise greater control over possession of castles, which in effect controlled the land. The construction of embattled secular buildings was regulated and from the 1190s the Crown issued licences to crenellate (embattle) the homes of barons who were considered trustworthy. On Henry II's accession in 1154 he found himself with control over few castles in East Anglia. In 1157 he forced Hugh Bigod, whose loyalty was suspect, to surrender his castles of Bungay, Framlingham, Thetford and Walton. Shortly after the first two were handed back in 1165, Henry began construction of a new stone castle on the coast at Orford. It has a keep which is circular internally but polygonal outside with three rectangular turrets. This stood inside a now-vanished curtain wall flanked by rectangular towers. This curtain wall formed a prototype for a larger towered enclosure built at Framlingham in the 1190s by the Bigods to refortify the castle which, like several others in East Anglia, was ordered destroyed by Henry II after the rebellion led by the king's sons in 1173-4. This was an early instance of a castle without a keep, all strength being concentrated on the curtain wall. Another castle of the same type but apparently fewer towers was built at Hadleigh in the 1230s, although by then the square towers used there were considered out of date, and other castles built in the Welsh Marches by Hubert de Burgh, then owner of Hadleigh, have round or D-shaped flanking towers. Round towers were used at the corners of the bailey wall built at Cambridge in the 1280s by Edward I, and also at Bungay at about the same period. These two castles had gateways set between pairs of D-shaped towers and Cambridge had a round tower keep set on the old motte. The castle at Norwich also once had late 13th century curtain walls with a twin-towered gatehouse. Clare is a fragment of a 13th century shell keep, a type where the original palisade around the lord's house on the motte was replaced by a stone wall against which lean-to buildings could be erected. Eye also seems to have had a keep of this sort, although the present structure on the mound dates from the 19th century. Structures of wood still remained in use, the palisade of the lower court at Framlingham being renewed in the 1290s.

*Castle Camps*

Also of the end of the 13th century is Woodcroft, a much smaller moated building where the curtain walls formed an integral part of four ranges of apartments around a small court, instead of enclosing free-standing or lean-to buildings as before. Just one range containing the gateway and having one round tower now remains. This formed the model for all the later castles of East Anglia. Apart from the moats, hardly anything now remains at Cheveley, Gresham and Morley, but single impressive fronts with central gatehouses survive from the 1340s at Mettingham and from the 1380s at Wingfield. Mettingham does not seems to have had corner towers, but it had some sort of private citadel for the lord, whilst at Wingfield there were two corner towers which were square, whilst the surviving two are octagonal, and the gatehouse has two semi-octagonal towers facing the field and fully octagonal stair turrets within. With their curtain walls pierced by large windows in the upper parts these buildings were more in the nature of fortified manor houses. This was even more true of two thinly walled mid 15th century examples at Baconsthorpe and Caister, and the possibly earlier Claxton. They were moated stronghouses, able to resist short lived assaults during French raids or local revolts, but not designed to withstand a full scale siege, although in 1469 a brave attempt was made to defend Caister from a siege by a hostile and overmighty neighbour. Possession of a high embattled tower was an important symbol of lordship and sometimes this was the most important reason for incorporating such a building otherwise of modest defensive strength. Caister has a very high circular corner tower and the halls at Baconsthorpe, Elton and Middleton have substantial gatehouses, whilst Faulkbourne Hall and Buckden Palace have impressive rectangular towers with corner turrets, those at Buckden rising the full height of the tower, whilst those at Faulkbourne are corbelled out near the top. These towers all contained suites of private rooms for the use of their respective lords.

East Anglia has a shortage of good building stone and Buckden, Caister, Claxton and Faulkbourne are built of brick, which had first been used in this sort of context at Little Wenham Hall, where, within a moat, an embattled chamber block was built onto a timber framed hall in the late 13th century. The block has a higher wing containing a small but fine chapel. This is a development on Weeting in which the lord's private part of the house is now distinguished by being taller, embattled, and of a different type of building material. At Longthorpe, near Peterborough, the stone chamber block has a more tower-like form, but no real military purpose. Chesterton Tower, near Cambridge, is another chamber block of this type, of just two storeys with fairly thin walls without battlements. The lodge at Thetford Warren also only had two storeys, and seems to have been self contained without an adjoining hall block.

A late 15th century brick building, Oxburgh Hall, marks the final transition from castle to the unfortified lordly house of the Tudor period. It has four thinly walled ranges set round a court. There are no towers and only the moat provided any real protection, but there is a very lofty gatehouse with octagonal corner turrets and a few cross-loops, more for show than for systematic defence by archery or handguns. The lord had chambers in one of the ranges, but the gatehouse upper rooms, being the most private and secure, were used by Henry VII when he paid a visit in 1492. The hall at Kirtling was similar but with a dry berm between the house and its moat.

Many manor houses in East Anglia were provided with moats in the 13th and 14th centuries. Some of them may be a response to periods of unrest during the reigns of Henry III and Edward II, but water-filled ditches were not necessarily military in purpose. A moat was a permanent and efficient boundary for keeping vagrants, wild animals and malefactors out of manorial enclosures, and would also have been equally useful for controlling the comings and goings of domestic animals, servants and members of the family. At all periods moats were appreciated as scenic features and they served as a habitat for fish, eels and water fowl, which together formed a substantial part of the diet of the land-owning classes. A wet moat could also help drain land otherwise unsuitable for agriculture or inhabitation. Moats were also used to flush away sewage so a house built within one would require a separate source of water for cooking, brewing and washing. Because of the many uses to which they were put, moats did not require royal consent of the kind which was supposed to be obtained (but not always was) for the erection of embattled walls and towers. They still had a function as status symbols since only those who held manors or a considerable share in one had the resources available to create them.

*Framlingham Castle*

*Tower house at Buckden*

*Gatehouse at Kirtling*

The words motte and moat clearly have a common origin and were once pronounced the same. Although modern historians normally understand them to mean different types of earthwork, in the medieval period this distinction was not so clear. One might expect a gradual development from the conical mounds and ringworks of the 11th and 12th centuries to the low quadrangular platforms which are the commonest type of moated site, although it is clear that rectangular platforms can be as early as the mid 12th century since King Stephen's castle at Burwell took that form. Quite a number of sites are hybrids, circular in form but with the internal platform not much raised above the surrounding ground.

Later medieval additions to 12th and 13th century castles in East Anglia are not widespread. Only buried foundations exist of domestic buildings at Castle Acre, Castle Rising, Hedingham and Pleshey, whilst those at Framlingham have been rebuilt almost out of existence. Edward III added several new round towers to Hadleigh in the 1360s, parts of which remain, although the domestic apartments of that period have almost vanished. A small fragment of a brick curtain wall probably of the same period survives at Castle Rising. It had a continuous series of lower embrasures forming an arcade, saving material and allowing firing loops at two levels. The walls built around the towns of King's Lynn, Great Yarmouth and Norwich were also built in this way. Long sections of the town walls at Yarmouth and Norwich still stand, with many circular and D-shaped towers, although King's Lynn (where much less of the walls remain) has the only surviving gatehouse, which is Tudor rather than medieval. Nothing remains of town walls at Ipswich, whilst those of Colchester were a remodelling of the old Roman walls, with one gateway of that period still surviving.

In the medieval period castle walls of rubble were sometimes limewashed outside, making them look very different from the way they appear today. Dressed stones around windows and doorways would be left uncovered. Domestic rooms would have had whitewashed rooms decorated with murals of biblical, historical or heroic scenes mostly painted in yellow and black. Longthorpe Tower has the finest set of domestic wall paintings now surviving in England. They date from the early 14th century. Not long after then wall hangings decorated with the same themes or heraldry came into fashion. Although used in churches, glass was expensive and uncommon in secular buildings before the 15th century, so windows were originally closed with wooden shutters. As a result rooms were dark when the weather was too cold or wet for the shutters to be opened for light and ventilation. In the later medieval period large openings in the outer walls sometimes had iron bars or grilles even if high above ground. Living rooms usually had fireplaces although some halls had central hearths with the smoke escaping through louvres in the roof. Latrines are commonly provided within the thickness of the walls and help to indicate which rooms were intended for living or sleeping in rather than just storage space. In the keeps at Norwich, Castle Rising and Orford groups of four latrines are placed on the same side of the building.

Furnishings were sparse up until the 15th century although the embrasures of upper storey windows often have built-in seats from the 13th century onwards. Lords with several castles tended to circulate around them administering their manorial courts and consuming agricultural produce on the spot. Castles belonging to great lords could be left almost empty when they were not in residence. For much of their lives castles gradually crumbled away with only a skeleton staff in residence to administer the estates. A full strength garrison would only be provided in times of unrest and at other times castles were only inhabited by administrative staff and perhaps by one or two knights owing castle guard duty as part of their land tenure agreement. Royal castles were often used by the sheriffs, whose personal armed retinue would provide basic security and guard prisoners and stocks of munitions. Servants and clerks travelled with their lords, as did portable furnishings such as rugs, wall-hangings, cooking vessels and bedding, all kept in wooden chests. The lord and his immediate family plus honoured guests and the senior household officials would enjoy a fair degree of privacy, having their own rooms. Servants and retainers enjoyed less comfort and privacy, sharing of beds and communal sleeping in the main hall and warm places of work like the kitchen and stables being common. The early castles had few private rooms but by the 14th century blocks of small rooms were common, and castles like Wingfield and Caister once had numerous private rooms.

*Gatehouse at Castle Rising*

*Remains of town walls at King's Lynn*

*Great Yarmouth Town Wall*

By the 16th century many of the older castles were abandoned ruins. The only surviving additions of that period are the chimneys which are relics of lost apartments at Framlingham, where the gateway was modified and provided with a barbican, the outer gatehouse at Baconsthorpe, and a timber-framed house built at Wingfield to replace the destroyed apartments. Henry VIII built forts along the Essex and Suffolk coasts to defend them against the anticipated foreign invasion after his break with the Roman church, but nothing now remains of any of them. The more important ones were replaced by larger forts later on. There is little to suggest castles in Norfolk and Suffolk saw much action during the Civil War of the 1640s, but the castle at Cambridge was remodelled with arrow-head shaped corner bastions by Parliament in 1643, and Colchester suffered a siege by Parliamentary troops in 1648.

Both the keeps at Colchester and Norwich continued to serve as prisons until the early 19th century. Eventually they were gutted inside and then re-roofed to serve as museums. At Castle Rising the main rooms of the keep were roofless by the mid 16th century but the kitchen and two rooms in the forebuilding remained in use and are still roofed. The keeps at Hedingham and Orford are also still floored and roofed, and remain almost unaltered, rare and valuable survivals. At Framlingham the curtain wall remains complete but the hall was rebuilt as a poor-house in the 16th and 17th centuries. Otherwise the principal survivals are the fortified houses, those at Buckden, Chesterton, Elton, Faulkbourne, Little Wenham, and Longthorpe and Oxburgh having remained habitable. Wingfield and Woodcroft are also still inhabited,

*Orford: Interior of keep*

although they are both much reduced from their medieval size. The fortified houses are mostly still private residences not open to the public but Oxburgh is now maintained by the National Trust, whilst English Heritage looks after Castle Rising, Framlingham, Longthorpe and Orford, open on payment of a fee. English Heritage also looks after Thetford Warren Lodge and the more fragmentary ruins at Baconsthorpe, Castle Acre, Hadleigh and Weeting, to which there is free access. Caister and Hedingham are also both open to the public, as is Stansted Mountfichet, a reconstruction of the 1980s on the original earthworks of what an 11th and 12th century wooden castle was like. The other sites are mostly now just earthworks, foundations or small fragments, and some earthworks are rather overgrown. Most of them are privately owned and there are houses within the sites of Castle Camps, Haughley and Mettingham, but there is free public access at all times to part or all of the earthworks of the motte and bailey castles at Cambridge, Clare, Ely, Rayleigh and Thetford.

# GLOSSARY OF TERMS

ASHLAR - Masonry of blocks with even faces & square edges. BAILEY - defensible space enclosed by a wall or a palisade and ditch. BARBICAN - defensible court or porch in front of an entrance. BARTIZAN - A turret corbelled out at the top of a wall, often at a corner. BASTION - A projection rising no higher than the curtain wall. BLOCKHOUSE - A free-standing tower or similar building designed to mount cannon. BRATTICE - A covered wooden gallery at the summit of a wall for defending its base. CORBEL - A projecting bracket supporting other stonework or timbers. CRENEL - A cit-away part of a parapet. CURTAIN WALL - A high enclosing stone wall around a bailey. EMBATTLED - provided with a parapet with indentations (crenellations). FOUR-CENTRED-ARCH - An arch drawn with four compass points, two on each side. JAMB - A side of a doorway, window or opening. KEEP - A citadel or ultimate strongpoint. The term is not medieval and such towers were then called donjons. LIGHT - A compartment of a window. LOOP - A small opening to admit light or for the discharge or missiles. MACHICOLATION - A slot for dropping or firing missiles at assailants. MERLONS - The upstanding portions of a parapet. MOAT - A defensive ditch, water filled or dry. MOTTE - A steep sided flat-topped mound, partly or wholly man-made. PARAPET - A wall for protection at any sudden drop. PELE or PEEL - Originally a palisaded court, later coming to mean a bastle or tower house. PLINTH - The projecting base of a wall. It may be battered (sloped) or stepped. PORTCULLIS - A wooden gate made to rise and fall in vertical grooves. POSTERN - A back entrance or lesser gateway. RINGWORK - An embanked enclosure of more modest size than a bailey, generally bigger but less high than a motte summit. SHELL KEEP - A small stone walled court built upon a motte or ringwork. SOLAR - A private living room for the lord and his family. TOWER HOUSE - Self contained defensible house with the main rooms stacked vertically. WALL-WALK - A walkway on top of a wall, always protected by a parapet. WARD - A stone walled defensive enclosure.

## PUBLIC ACCESS TO THE SITES   Codes used in the gazetteers.

E   Buildings in the care of English Heritage. Fee payable at some sites.
F   Buildings to which there is free access at any time.
H   Buildings currently used as hotels, restaurants, shops, etc.
O   Buildings opened to the public by private owners, local councils, trusts.
V   Buildings closely visible from public roads, paths, churchyards & open spaces.

## FURTHER READING

Victoria County Histories of the counties of Cambridge, Huntingdon,
    Northamptonshire (for the soke of Peterborough) and Suffolk
R.C.A.H.M. Inventories of ancient monuments for Cambridgeshire and Essex
Norman Castles in Britain, Derek Renn, 1968
Castles from the Air, R. Allen Brown, 1989
Castellarium Anglicanum, David Cathcart King, 1983
Discovering Castles in Eastern England, John Kinross, 1968
Cambridge, Essex, Norfolk and Suffolk each have their own archeological and
    antiquarian societies which publish annual proceedings. See also periodicals such
    as Fortress, Medieval Archeology, Archeological Journal, and Country Life.
Guide pamphlets or histories are available for Baconsthorpe, Buckden, Buckenham,
    Bungay, Burgh, Caister, Castle Acre, Castle Rising, Colchester, Framlingham,
    Hadleigh, Hedingham, Longthorpe, North Elmham, Norwich, Orford, Oxburgh, and
    Stansted Mountfichet.

# CASTLES OF CAMBRIDGESHIRE

## ALDRETH CASTLE

The site of the castle erected by William I in 1071 to curtail the activities of Hereward the Wake has not been identified for certain. In 1140 the castle was repaired by Nigel, Bishop of Ely, but it was soon captured by King Stephen. In 1143 it was captured by Geoffrey de Mandeville, Earl of Essex.

## BASSINGBOURNE CASTLE   TL 325451

In 1266 Warin de Bassingbourn was licensed by Henry III to enclose his house here with a dyke and a wall of stones and to crenellate it. He died only two years later and it is doubtful as to how much he actually managed to build. The site is now referred to as "John of Gaunt's house". All that remains are mostly ploughed-out earthworks with a inner platform about 40m by 35m within the north end of a large outer enclosure 120m by 90m which still has a water-filled ditch on the south, where the ditch has a curved layout as if for bastions flanking the outer gateway. A bridge abutment remained visible until removed in 1887.

## BOURN CASTLE   TL 322561

Bourn Hall lies in the middle of an enclosure 130m across defined by a ditch which is still water filled on the SE, where there is a rampart, and there are traces of a smaller enclosure to the NE. These earthworks seem too large and weak to form part of a normal ringwork and bailey type castle but have generally been assumed to mark the site of the castle of Picot of Cambridge, who held Bourn in 1086. He gave "the church of Brune and the chapel of the castle" to a priory founded at Cambridge which later moved to Barnwell. In 1138 the castle was held against King Stephen by William Peverel. According to Camden the castle was burnt in 1264 by Ribald de Lisle.

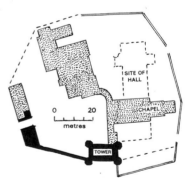

*Plan of Buckden Palace*

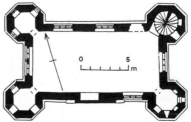

*Buckden Palace*

*Plan of tower at Buckden*

# BUCKDEN PALACE    TL 193677    V

Immediately north of the parish church lies the former palace of the Bishops of Lincoln, now used by the Claretians. It was once surrounded by a wet moat and has on the south side a brick tower house begun by Bishop Thomas Rotherham (1472-80) and completed by Bishop John Russell (1480-94), whose arms formerly appeared on woodwork inside. A length of low curtain wall with a wall-walk over a series of closely-spaced embrasures forming an arcade runs off from the tower to join up with an office on the south side of a west facing gatehouse, these parts being the work of Bishop Russell. The gatehouse has diagonal buttresses at all four corners and a stair to two upper storeys in a turret on the north side. The gatehouse, curtain and tower were show pieces designed to impress visitors arriving through the outer court to the SW, where a gateway survives, rather than as serious fortification. The Great Tower measures 15m by 7.5m and has octagonal corner turrets rising above the main building. The NE turret contains a staircase rising from the adjacent entrance on the north side to serve two upper storeys and the battlements. There is also a basement below courtyard level. The other turrets contain small rooms. The tower has three light windows even at courtyard level, where there is a fireplace in a projecting breast on the south side, and the walls are barely a metre thick so the tower is in fact no more of a fortress than any of the many 16th century gatehouses with the same plan, although it certainly looks very impressive from the outside. Blue bricks are used to make patterns on the wall contrasting with the background red.

NE of the Great Tower and east of a modern Catholic church is a chapel built by Bishop John Williams (1621-42) standing on the site of the west end of a medieval chapel. Between here and the Great Tower was a great chamber. Bishop Hugh de Wells (1209-35) is said to have erected a manor house at Buckden and Bishop Robert Grosseteste, who died here in 1254, may have built the hall and had the moat dug. The brick foundations of a hall 25m long internally with porches near the north end which have been revealed were probably of Bishop Rotherham's time. After her marriage to Henry VIII was annulled in 1533, Catherine of Aragon was sent to Buckden Palace. The locals supported her and threatened the Duke of Suffolk, when he was sent to move her, although she was eventually transferred to Kimbolton. Many of the buildings were demolished in the 1650s but in the 1660s Bishop Robert Sanderson patched up the remnants to make a dwelling. The existing house is of 1872. North of the palace lay a small park enclosed by a wall with a raised walk inside it, and an orchard lies to the SE, both parts having fishponds in them.

*Curtain wall and tower house at Buckden*

*Gatehouse at Buckden*

## BURWELL CASTLE    TL 587661    F

Burwell was one of several castles begun in 1143 by King Stephen to control Geoffrey de Mandeville, Earl of Essex. Geoffrey was mortally wounded whilst besieging the still unfinished castle in 1144. Excavations have shown it was never completed, since Geoffrey's death removed the need for a strongpoint here. The site lies on the north side of a stream which fed a wet moat up to 40m wide around a platform 95m long by 50m wide. Footings of a curtain wall were found on the east and south sides, together with a square gate tower with diagonal buttresses facing east towards the field. The buttresses (and perhaps all the walling) date from the 14th century, when the site was re-occupied and had a chapel amongst its buildings.

## CAMBRIDGE CASTLE    TL 446593    F

According to Domesday Book (1086) twenty-seven houses were removed to make room for the castle which William I ordered erected on the north bank of the river here in 1068. It had a large motte and two baileys. Henry II had the castle repaired in 1156-9, and spent £31 on it in 1172, whilst £50 was spent on works at the beginning of Richard I's reign. King John spent over £200 on the hall and chamber in 1212-16 so parts, at least, of the castle must have been of stone by then. In 1216 the castle was captured by rebel barons in league with Prince Louis of France. In 1283 Edward I began a rebuilding of the castle with new curtain walls with round flanking towers at the NW, NE and east corners, a twin-towered gatehouse on the SW and a round tower keep on the motte at the south end, the works costing £2,525, and including water filled moats protecting both the mound and the bailey. The walls were in need of repair by 1367 and during the 15th and 16th centuries stone was taken from the site for erecting college buildings. The gatehouse long remained in use as a prison and the curtain wall was maintained enough to enclose the court, although in 1590 the castle was described as "old, ruined and decayed".

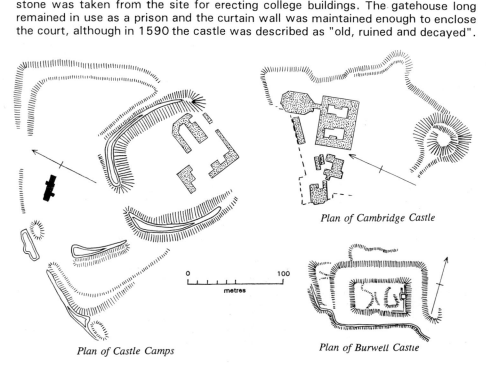

Plan of Cambridge Castle

0    100
metres

Plan of Castle Camps

Plan of Burwell Castle

*Motte at Cambridge*

In 1643 the bailey was modified into a fort with angular bastions. Fifteen houses were cleared out of the way and the great hall was replaced by a brick barrack block. The new defences were dismantled by Parliament in 1647 but the gatehouse and barracks remained in use as a prison. The bailey was lowered and levelled and the moat between it and the motte filled in when a new octagonal County gaol was erected in 1802-7. A Shire Hall of 1932 now stands on the site of this in the northern half of the bailey site. The gatehouse survived until 1842 when it was demolished to make way for a courthouse which was demolished in 1954. The motte still survives in a slightly altered state with modern terracing, and there are traces of the east and north bastions of the 17th century fort, the west bastion having been destroyed in 1811. The town was protected by a ditch on the south and east sides, probably of Saxon origin but recut and made wider and provided with two gates in the 13th century. The "King's Ditch" is shown on Richard Lyne's map of 1574.

## CARLTON: LOPHAM'S HALL    TL 647521

The hall lies in the middle of an egg-shaped platform 90m long which was surrounded by a ditch over 20m wide, now mostly filled in.

## CASTLE CAMPS    TL 627424    F

A farmhouse (not accessible to the public) now occupies part of a ringwork about 90m across built in 1068 by Aubrey de Vere. The earthwork is levelled on the west but the other sides still have a deep ditch with water in the bottom of it. In the 19th century a bridge over the moat was replaced by a wide causeway. The very large outer enclosure to the east and south, in which lies the church, probably dates from the late 13th century when the castle was much improved by the de Vere earls of Oxford. A curved pool lying within the west part seems to be a remnant of the original much more modestly sized outer bailey. In 1526 there was a quarrel over possession between a dowager countess and the then new earl. Edward, Earl of Oxford sold the castle in 1584 to the London merchant Thomas Skynner. An old print shows a substantial house of about that period adjoining a four storey tower with large mullioned windows on the top two levels. The property later passed through various hands before being given to Charterhouse School in 1611.

## CAXTON CASTLE   TL 294587

A platform 60m long by 30m wide is surrounded by a deep ditch still containing water. The ditch around a second platform of similar size on the south side is now dry. There is an outer moat on the north and a small moated outer enclosure on the east. The site does not appear to have any recorded history.

## CHESTERTON TOWER   TL 464598

This mid 14th century building is thought to have been the residence of a canon of Vercelli Abbey. The connection with the Italian monastery was severed later and in 1440 Chesterton was given by Henry VI to King's Hall, which later became Trinity College. The tower contained a living room over a room with a fine rib-vault in two bays which probably served as an office, since it has two-light windows. A north turret contains a spiral stair, the west turret contains an octagonal room over a small closet, and the south projection contains a latrine. The SE side has a chimney stack.

## CHEVELEY CASTLE   TL 678613

A platform 50m by 40m surrounded by a ditch up to 25m wide remain of a castle which Sir John de Pulteney, one time Mayor of London, was licensed to crenellate by Edward III in 1341. The site is entered by a causeway at the NW end. There are slight traces of the outer wall and footings of a round tower which did not project much outside the enceinte.

## DIDDINGTON MOAT   TL 198647

The moated platform may be the site of the castle of Southoe or Boughton first mentioned in 1140 but abandoned by 1153.

## ELTON HALL   TL 088930

The oldest parts of this building are the late 15th century gatehouse and the vaulted undercroft of the chapel which both form part of the SE range of what is assumed to have been a quadrangular mansion with a hall in the NW range. This work was begun by Sir Richard Sapcote and probably completed by his son Sir John. Both parts have a projecting bay, that of the gatehouse having clasping buttresses which form turrets at the level of the machicolated parapet. The side arches of this bay are 17th century insertions. A four-centred arch leads into a passage with quadripartite vaulting. The house was sold in 1617 and was ruinous by the 1660s when Sir Thomas Proby dismantled parts of it and built a three storey embattled block beyond the chapel and a wing extending a right-angles to it forming a SW range. In the 18th century the SW range was doubled in width and two round turrets added to the SW end of the SE range, which was itself doubled in width in the 1850s except for the part beside the gatehouse.

## EATON SOCON CASTLE   TL 173588

The overgrown earthworks on the west bank of the Ouse comprise a south bailey 55m long by 50m wide with high ramparts except on the side facing the river, a ramparted north bailey 66m long by 35m wide and an outer bailey on the west. Excavations showed evidence of the site being occupied from Saxon times until the late medieval period and that the ditch was revetted with beech planking.

*Motte at Huntingdon*

## ELY CASTLE    TL 541799    F

The overgrown motte 12m high known as Cherry Hill lies in private grounds but the worn banks of the bailey to the SE lie in a public open space. The motte is about 16m across on top whilst the bailey measures about 90m across each way. The castle was built in 1071 by William I, and was refortified in 1140 by Bishop Nigel, much to the disgust of his monks, but was soon captured along with the Isle of Ely by King Stephen. The castle in which Faulkes de Breaute and other royalists shut themselves up in 1215 may have been at the west end of the Isle of Ely, since according to Bentham a windmill stood on top of Cherry Hill by 1229.

## GREAT STAUGHTON CASTLE    TL 116630

In the middle of a large enclosure with a wet moat is a round platform with its own wet moat.

## HARTFORD CASTLE    TL 248755

The low oval motte has a counterscarp bank beyond the wet moat. The bailey also has a wet moat.

## HUNTINGDON CASTLE    TL 242715    F

Of a castle erected by William I in 1068 there remain on the north bank of the River Ouse mutilated earthworks of a large but low motte and a bailey with a substantial east rampart. The bypass crosses the site of a second bailey west of the motte. The 3m high mound 350km to the west beside the Mill stream is likely to be the siege castle erected in 1174 by Richard de Lucy, the Justiciar. David, Earl of Huntingdon, surrendered the castle after his brother William the Lion, King of Scotland, was captured at Alnwick and it was then demolished by order of Henry II, with "hooks, crooks and axes". Foundations are said to have been located of a stone gatehouse but there is nothing to suggest the site ever had stone curtain walls nor was it re-fortified, but a 17th century windmill stood on the mound until 1912. The town was fortified in the Saxon period but no defences now remain from that era or later.

## KIMBOLTON CASTLE    TL 094674 & 100677

The original castle of the Mandevilles in this district stood on a wet moated motte. The castle mentioned in 1217 probably stood on the present site to the NE, and it was presumably this building which was captured in 1221 during the short-lived rebellion of William de Forz, Count of Aumale. It is also mentioned in documents of 1275, 1364 and 1373, when it was held by the Montague family, and it is known to have once had a double moat. The castle was remodelled in the 1520s and was inhabited by the divorced former queen Catherine of Aragon in 1536. It was rebuilt in 1617-20 with four ranges around a court. In 1707 the SE corner of the house collapsed and between then and 1714 the Duke of Manchester had the present house erected to a design by Vanbrugh. It incorporates a few 16th century windows but there are no obvious medieval parts now remaining.

## KIRTLING TOWERS    TL 685575    V

Of the early 16th century mansion of the North family there remains only the lofty brick gatehouse with polygonal corner turrets and a four-centred arch with a two-storey oriel above. The rest was demolished in 1801 and a modest house was erected beside the gatehouse c1850. Behind the gatehouse is a platform where the rest of the mansion lay. Surrounding the whole is an outer enclosure 120m by 140m with a ditch which has been filled in on the south but still contains a 20m width of water on the east side and a narrower moat on the north. If the west arm of the moat contained water a dam would have been needed since the bottom here is at a higher level. A castle here forming the seat of a barony is referred to in 1219. On Robert de Tony's death in 1309 the castle is specifically described as having a palisade and moat, whilst in 1336 it was a "forcelettum" held by William de la Zouch, who had married the Tony heiress. In 1260 three men were carrying a cask of wine across the bridge (probably a drawbridge) of the castle when it collapsed under their weight.

Longthorpe Tower

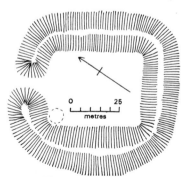

Plan of Cheveley Castle

2nd STOREY

3rd STOREY

Longthorpe: plans

## KNAPWELL MOTTE    TL 337632

Saxo-Norman pottery has been discovered on the mound near the church.

## LONGTHORPE TOWER    TL 163984    E

In 1263 Sir William Thorpe obtained permission from Robert, Abbot of Peterborough to rebuild the parochial chapel of St Botolph on a more convenient site. The present church was built in consequence and a new house was then erected not far west of it. The impressive tower containing a new great chamber is assumed to have been added by Robert Thorpe, appointed Steward of the abbey in 1310. His son Robert, Steward of the abbey from 1330, probably commissioned the wall-paintings in the great chamber. Two other members of this family achieved prominence during the second half of Edward III's reign, Sir William, who became Lord Chief Justice but lost his estates after being impeached for bribery, and Sir Robert, who became Chancellor. The Thorpe estates passed to John Wyttilbury in 1391, and Longthorpe passed about a century later to the Fitzwilliams of Milton. In 1947 Earl Fitzwilliam placed Longthorpe Tower in State care. English Heritage are now the custodians.

The tower now lies within the suburbs of Peterborough. It measures 8.5m square over walls 1.8m thick and rises 12m through three storeys up to a wall walk with a plain parapet with raised corners. SW of the tower is a thinly walled block which presumably contained a hall over offices or stores. It has one good late 13th century two-light window in the north end wall. On the east side is a modern extension, and on the west is a 17th century wing which contained a kitchen at ground level. These parts are not open to the public, who enter the tower by wooden steps up to a doorway on the east side, converted from a former window, from which leads a passage to a room in the SE corner. The rib-vaulted room at this level was the great chamber or lord's private room, and was entered by a narrow passage from the hall NE corner. The west wall contained an arched recess with a small window and originally there was the same arrangement on the north side. However the tower soon showed signs of structural instability (it is badly cracked now) and the north recess was then filled in except for a window embrasure. A stair in the south wall leads up to the bedroom above. This room has a window in each wall, that on the south having a latrine (in a destroyed overhanging projection) and the stair to the roof leading off its embrasure. The windows have shouldered lintels indicating a date c1300-20 and were closed by shutters secured with draw-bars. The lowest level, also rib-vaulted, was a store without any means of communication with the upper levels. For this reason the tower is to be regarded basically as a status symbol rather than a serious piece of fortification.

The wall paintings were discovered under many top coats of limewash by the then tenant Hugh Horrell in 1946. For completeness and quality they have no parallel in any medieval domestic building in Britain, although paintings of this type must have once been common. They are now mostly red and yellow although tests have shown that there were other colours which have faded. On the north wall is a Nativity scene with the Seven Ages of Man above. Below is a series of Apostles starting in the west window recess and going right round to the east embrasure. Over the fireplace in the east wall is the Wheel of the Five Senses, a subject mentioned in a manuscript but not illustrated anywhere else. Above is a man with his dog. The scheme on the south wall is well preserved and purely secular. There are various figures including what are probably Edward II and Edward III and several sets of heraldic arms. The top part of the west wall has scenes of the Labours of the Months and a selection of birds. The vault has figures of musicians and symbols of the Four Evangelists.

# RAMPTON MOAT   TL 431681

NW of Rampton bridge is a platform about 50m by 40m with a ditch over 30m wide still partly containing water. The platform is dominated by an outer bank beyond the moat on the north side, and is reached by a causeway at the SW corner. It is likely that this is one of the castles King Stephen erected against Geoffrey de Mandeville in 1143 and it was left incomplete after Geoffrey's death the following year.

# WISBECH CASTLE   TF 462096

This castle was erected in 1071 by William I. It was damaged by flooding in 1236, and it was attacked in 1350 by a party of men disputing the Bishop of Ely's jurisdictional powers in the area. Bishop Morton improved the accommodation in the 1480s and the castle was later used as a royal prison, the gunpowder plotter Catesby being held within it in 1605. There are no remains but a plan of 1794 shows a circular enclosure.

# WOODCROFT CASTLE   TF 140045

Only the three storey west range and the wet moat now survive of a quadrangular mansion of c1300. Characteristic of that date are the windows with shouldered lintels in the thinly-walled round tower 5.5m in external diameter projecting at the NW corner. This tower has three storeys with a latrine recess on the second level. The west range has in the middle a poorly defended gateway flanked by rooms for a porter and guard and having a room which was formerly a chapel above it. Otherwise the internal arrangements have been much altered. Originally there was a tower at the SE corner and perhaps others at the east corners. The hall presumably lay in the east range. During Charles I's reign Woodcroft was inhabited by his chaplain Dr Hudson, who escaped from confinement by Cromwell in the Tower of London and fortified the castle, although it can hardly have been strong enough to resist contemporary cannon. He was promised quarter upon his surrender but was cut down while clinging to a gargoyle. The soldier who dragged him out of the moat is said to have subsequently displayed Dr Hudson's tongue as a trophy.

# WOOD WALTON CASTLE   TL 211828

There are slight traces of earthworks on a low hill of a castle built c1144 by Ernulf de Mandeville, son of the infamous Geoffrey, Earl of Essex.

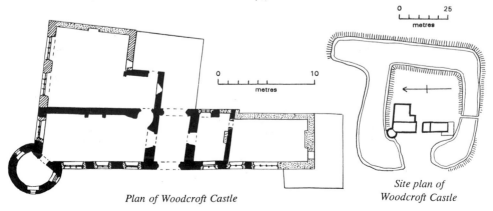

*Plan of Woodcroft Castle*

*Site plan of Woodcroft Castle*

# CASTLES OF ESSEX

## BERDEN RINGWORKS    TL 470289 & TL 466292

There are small ringworks at Stock's Farm and the Rookery. The latter has a wet ditch and may be the earlier of the two. Excavation found little evidence of occupation and no sign of a palisade. Perhaps it was left incomplete and abandoned in favour of the other site.

## BIRCH CASTLE    TL 943198

There are only slight traces of earthworks now remaining.

## BOCKING MOTTE    TL 764278

This is a low overgrown motte with a ditch 3m deep containing water at the bottom.

## CHRISHALL MOTTE    TL 452386

This is a small overgrown motte with a surrounding moat 3m deep.

## CLAVERING CASTLE    TL 471319    V

North of the churchyard and rather oddly commanded by it is a platform about 80m by 50m defended by a deep ditch which on the north side is over 20m wide and 5m deep and still contains water. On this side there is an outer bank and various other earthworks beyond. Clavering belonged to Robert Fitz Wymarc during Edward the Confessor's reign and has been identified with the Robert's Castle mentioned in 1052, but Great Canfield seems a more likely candidate. Clavering is generally considered to have been a stone castle and the site would have been difficult to defend without a stone curtain wall, but there are no remains of a curtain wall nor are there any certain historical references to the site.

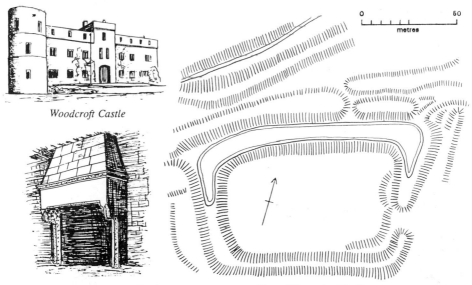

Woodcroft Castle

Fireplace in Woodcroft Castle

Plan of Clavering Castle

## COLCHESTER CASTLE   TL 999253   O

The Roman town walls of Camulodunum must have remained defensible in the 11th century, and much of the circuit still survives today in a reduced and defaced condition, but despite this the town was captured and burnt in a Danish attack of 1071. There is no record of the erection of the castle but a charter of Henry I granting custody of it to his steward, Eudo, mentions use of it by both William I and William II, so the keep is assumed to have been begun c1075-80 to dominate this important town and help defend it against another attack. The bailey defended by a substantial rampart and ditch to the north and east of the keep may be contemporary with it or could be the bailey created by Henry II after the rebellion of 1172-3. The walls were repaired in 1182. The constableship was long held by the de Lanvalei family but King John distrusted them and took possession of the castle, strengthening it and leaving it under the command of the Flemish mercenary Stephen Harengoot. The castle was restored to the Lanvelei family as part of the terms of Magna Carta, but in 1216 King John captured the castle without much resistance. Later that year the castle was handed over to Prince Louis of France as part of a truce agreement.

The castle saw little subsequent use except as a prison, being first mentioned in this role in 1226. In 1429 the Lollard William Chieveling was imprisoned in the castle prior to being burnt in front of it. During Queen Mary's reign twenty three "heretics" (Protestants), were burnt in the town. The last martyr to be imprisoned in the castle was the Quaker James Parnell, arrested for preaching to large crowds in 1655. Although officially recorded that he starved himself to death, he died because the gaoler Nicholas Roberts did not allow food brought by friends to reach him. In 1645 Matthew Hopkins, the self-styled "Witch-Finder General" used the castle as his base. In it he tortured unfortunate women into confessing to acts of witchcraft, denying them sleep and pricking them with a needle to try and find their "witch's mark" where they felt no pain. In 1648 Colchester was seized by a Royalist force which had been driven away from London. Sir Thomas Fairfax besieged them for seventy-six days until they surrendered in August. Two Royalist leaders, Sir Charles Lucas and Sir George Lisle, were imprisoned in the keep until executed by firing squad, a stone outside marking the spot where they died, whilst the unfortunate townsfolk, left with little food or fuel during the siege, were fined £12,000 for harbouring the enemy.

*The keep at Colchester*

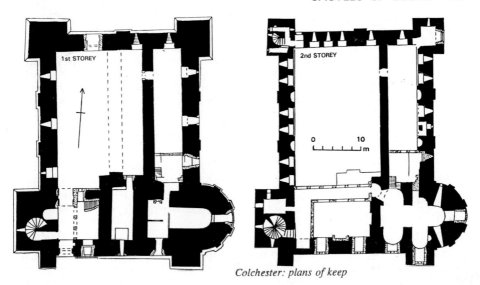

*Colchester: plans of keep*

The castle ceased to be the county gaol in 1668 but the rooms in the SE corner still served as the town prison until 1835. John Wheeley, a local ironmonger, acquired the castle in 1683 and tried to demolish it for the materials. It was then that the Roman vaults underneath were discovered. Only the top part of the walls were destroyed before the attempt was given up. In 1727 the castle was given as a wedding present to the lawyer Charles Grey. He had the southern end of the upper storey made habitable again as a library. John Howard, the prison reformer, was appalled by conditions for prisoners here. Just prior to one visit in 1775 even the head gaoler had died of typhus caused by poor sanitation. The castle passed to the Round family in 1782 and was sold by them to the borough in 1920. The ruined parts were re-roofed in the 1930s to protect further deterioration to the Roman vaults, into which water was seeping. Since 1938 the keep has served as the town museum.

Probably because of a shortage of building materials in this district the castle keep re-uses a lot of Roman material and was built upon the foundations of a Roman temple of Claudius. The keep thus stands in the middle of the Roman town rather than against the outer walls. In AD 60 Queen Boudica rose up against the Romans and attacked the then unfortified town, whose inhabitants took refuge in the temple. After two days it was stormed and everyone inside was slaughtered.

Measuring 46m by 33m over walls 3.3m thick, the Colchester keep is by far the largest Norman keep in existence. There are large turrets clasping the NE and NW corners, slightly smaller projections at each end of the south wall, and a larger rectangular turret at the south end of the west wall which contains the main spiral staircase with steps no less than 2.3m wide, plus a chamber beside it on the upper storey. Rising from the boldly battered plinth are pilaster buttresses on the west, north and east sides, plus a more closely spaced series of four pilasters on the 12m diameter apse projecting at the south end of the east wall. How high the keep once stood above the present two storeys is a matter of controversy but comparison with the similarly planned White Tower at London makes it clear that a third storey was intended. On the upper storey the SE corner of the Colchester keep has what is usually interpreted as an under-chapel with apses facing east and two each to north and south. The assumption is that an aisled chapel similar to the one at London was intended above this on the third storey, but if built it was dismantled in the 1690s.

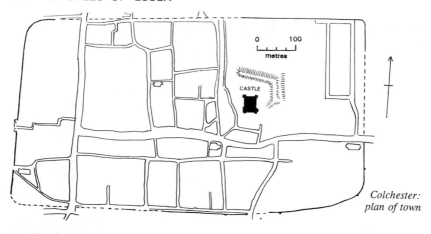

*Colchester:*
*plan of town*

Blocked up battlements visible halfway up the wall outside suggest that the lowest storey was built quickly and then made defensible as soon as possible. The upper storey may not have been added until the early 12th century, and the doorway of four orders with roll-mouldings and a billet motif leading directly into the basement at the SW corner could have been inserted then. Certainly it is hard to accept this doorway as being as early as c1080, especially since it has a portcullis groove. Few Norman keeps had portcullises and there are no other buildings earlier than the 1130s known to have had one. A portcullis was perhaps provided here since there was no forebuilding with steps up to a second storey entrance as was usual in Norman keeps. Later in the 12th century a small forebuilding was provided and in the 13th century a small court or barbican was built around it with a loopholed wall and round turrets flanking a gateway. Footings of it remain under the access bridge, and to the east of it is the base of a late 11th century apsed chapel, possibly a few years older than the keep. To the south there once lay a hall. A penny of Henry I was found in the bailey rampart, which is actually the old temple precinct wall robbed of its useful core-stones and buried within an earth bank.

Internally the keep upper storey contained a huge hall divided by a crosswall with one doorway from a long narrow private chamber with two fireplaces. The crosswall has many reused Roman tiles laid in a herringbone pattern, originally hidden under plaster. The southern half of the private chamber has a latrine and may have been partitioned off. At this level the NE turret contains a square room, whilst the NW turret contained two latrines and a staircase rising up from the hall. The hall has six window embrasures on the west side, divided into three pairs by two fireplaces. The arrangement of the four north facing windows suggests the eastern part of the hall had an arcade, and a subdivision here would have been necessary to span the hall, which was no less than 18m wide. The lower storey certainly shows signs of having had a wall or arcade in this position. The lower rooms were dark storerooms with few windows. The chamber next to the entrance contains a well and has access into the vaults of the Roman temple underneath. During World War II these vaults were used as an air raid shelter. East of the well chamber are the various rooms long used as prisons. In the 18th century renovation rooms were closed off at the south end of the private chamber and the level below but otherwise the hall and chamber and the storerooms below them were left open to the sky until re-roofed and floored in the 1930s. The upper rooms at the south end have 18th century mullioned windows. Also of that period are the top room of the NE turret which Charles Grey used as a study and the cupola over the top of the main staircase.

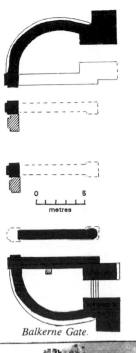

Balkerne Gate.

The keep, Colchester

Old Print of Faulkbourne Hall

Balkerne Gate, Colchester

The 2nd century Roman walls of the town enclose a rectangle 900m long by 450m wide perched on a hill. They were 2.6m thick and were of concrete with a stone facing with brick bonding courses. At the corners and intervals along the sides were square towers projecting internally into the bank backing onto the walls. In the 13th century the walls were strengthened by adding six or seven external-projecting round bastions, four of which survive. Considerable parts remain of the Balkerne Gate at the west end, one of the largest of its type in Roman Britain, being 32m long with a projection of 9m in front of the wall. It had two 5m wide archways for wheeled traffic flanked outside by a pair of 2m wide entrances for pedestrians. Two archways survive together with the quadrant-shaped flanking towers, that on the north still being 4.5m high. The gateway was remodelled after a fire in the 4th century and was partly blocked up in late Saxon times.

*Interior of keep at Colchester before restoration*

# EAST MERSEA FORT    TM 072153

Henry VIII had a triangular-shaped artillery fort begun here shortly before he died in 1547. It was captured during the Royalist uprising of 1648.

# ELMDON RINGWORK    TL 460400

The ringwork at Castle Grove rises 6m to a summit 27m by 20m. Part of it has slipped down into the surrounding ditch.

# FAULKBOURNE HALL    TL 803166

In 1439 Henry VI licensed Sir John Montgomery to crenellate his house at Faulkbourne. Until then the main building was a timber-framed hall, but Sir John rebuilt it in brick. The hall is assumed to have largely attained its present appearance by 1489, when Henry VII proposed to stay in it. The result is an impressive building two rooms deep with staircases in the central east-west spine. The southern half still contains some timber-framed parts earlier than the 1430s but encased with brick and with the cross-wing at the east end provided with two polygonal bay windows. The original hall was replaced by a new hall on the north side. At the NW and SW corners are towers 4.8m across with their corners canted off to north and south, but not towards the west. There is a smaller bay in the middle of the north front. At the NE corner is a three storey tower 7.5m square with a staircase in an octagonal SE turret, and polygonal tourelles set upon diagonal buttresses at the NE and NW corners, whilst there are cross-loops in the corbelled-out parapet. The tower has thin walls and its lowest level was a private living room with pairs of two-light windows a fireplace on the north side rising in a corbelled out breast (for the room is considerable above the ground level outside). So this tower was intended to an impressive show-piece but was not really capable of being defended. See old print on page 27.

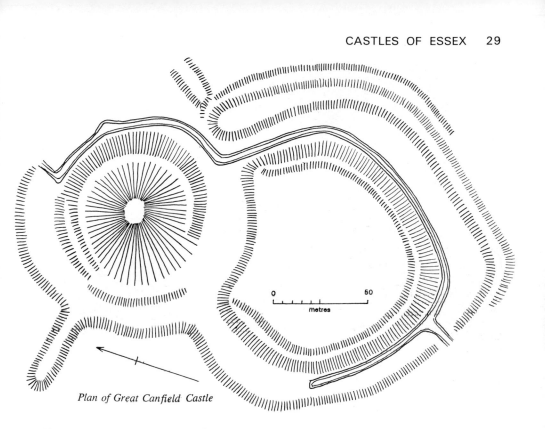

*Plan of Great Canfield Castle*

## GREAT CANFIELD CASTLE    TL 594179

Although it does not appear to have ever had stone defences, this castle has some impressive earthworks and was formerly a place of considerable man-made strength. The mound rises 14m from a ditch which still contains water on the east side to a summit 10m across. The horseshoe shaped bailey south of it measures 90m across and has a substantial rampart and a ditch still containing water for much of the circuit. Originally a higher level of water was held in by an outer bank on the east and west sides. To the west lay a still larger outer bailey with a more modest ditch about 9m wide, although there is a wider pool of water at the west corner. The castle was probably built by Robert fitz Wymarc, who came over to England with King Edward the Confessor in 1042. It seems a more likely candidate than Clavering for the "Robert's Castle" to which the "Frenchmen" at Edward's court fled when Earl Godwin returned from exile in 1052.

## GREAT EASTON    TL 608254

A rectangular moated platform was built in the 13th or 14th century into the site of the rectangular bailey of an earlier castle with a motte 6m high. Excavations in the bailey in 1964 produced 11th and 12th century pottery.

## GREAT ILFORD    TQ 437852

The small mound known as Lavender Mount is probably the remains of a motte. It adjoins a very large enclosure, more suited to a village than as a bailey.

*Hadleigh Castle*

# HADLEIGH CASTLE   TQ 810861   F

The manor of Hadleigh was held by Hubert de Burgh, Justiciar of England and Earl of Kent, during King John's reign, but it was not until 1230 that he and his wife Margaret obtained a licence from Henry III to build a castle there. It was still incomplete when de Burgh fell from favour in 1232, but the king decided to complete the castle as a royal stronghold. In the 1360s Edward III remodelled both the defences and the royal apartments. Documents mention the great hall, the king's chamber and wardrobe, the queen's chamber and both an old chapel and a new one. The castle was sometimes assigned to queen consorts as part of their dower, both Edward I and Edward II doing this. Henry VIII gave the castle successively to Catherine of Aragon, Anne of Cleves and Catherine Parr. Anne, who "spoke only German and spent her time chiefly in needlework" lived at Hadleigh following her divorce. The castle fell into ruin after being sold by Edward VI to Lord Riche in 1551. It has been in state care as an ancient monument since 1948, and is now maintained by English Heritage.

The castle stands on the edge of an escarpment above the Leigh Marshes by the Thames estuary. Unfortunately the ground has proved unstable and the whole south side lies in fragments scattered around at all angles on the slope. The court measures 100m long by 70m wide and was surrounded by a wall 2m thick with the very unusual feature of closely spaced pilaster buttresses on the inner face. Most of this wall is now reduced to within 2m of the ground. The only surviving 13th century towers lie on the west side, one at the NW corner by a postern being 5m square, another at the now collapsed SW corner being 6m square, with a rectangular tower between them that perhaps contained latrines for the solar block at the south end of a hall on this side. Such small square towers are unusual for this period, when larger round towers were the norm. Excavations have shown that later in the 13th century a smaller new hall was built immediately east of the site of the old one, with blocks of apartments at each end of it.

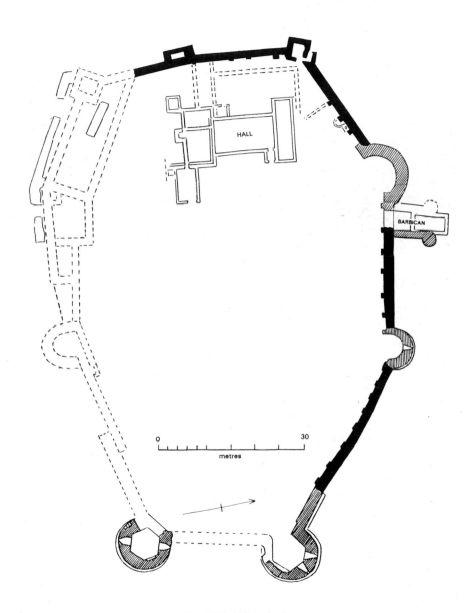

HALL

BARBICAN

0              30

metres

*Plan of Hadleigh Castle*

*Hadleigh Castle*

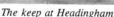

*The keep at Headingham*

*Hadleigh: plan of SE Tower*

The most impressive part of the present ruin is the circular SE tower 10m in diameter above a battered plinth, which contained two upper storeys of fine polygonal chambers with latrines and fireplaces above a basement. This tower and its much more ruinous twin at the NE corner, now leaning to the south, formed part of the mid 14th century remodelling of the castle. At the same time slightly smaller D-shaped towers were added on the north and south sides, a large new chamber block was built in the SW corner of the court, and a barbican was built to defend the gateway facing NW. The barbican had twin D-shaped turrets at the north end and enclosed a drawbridge-pit. Immediately to the west is the lower part of a tower 14m in diameter, probably the great tower mentioned in old documents, although since the part of it that stood within the court is entirely destroyed it now looks more like a D-shaped bastion. Beside the curtain wall at this point stood the kitchen.

## HARWICH FORTS

Nothing now remains of three artillery forts or blockhouses built to defend the harbour by Henry VIII in 1539. They were known as the Middle House or Bulwark, the Bulwark upon the Hill, and the Blockhouse of the Tower. Edward III licensed the construction of town defences in 1352 but there does not appear to be any evidence that anything was ever actually built.

*Interior of the court room in the keep at Hedingham*

## HEDINGHAM CASTLE    TL 787358    O

The earthworks here are likely to go back to the late 11th century when Hedingham was held by the first Aubrey de Vere. His son Aubrey II served Henry I and Stephen as Chamberlain and was killed in a London riot in 1141, possibly because his daughter Rohesia was married to the unpopular Geoffrey de Mandeville, Earl of Essex. In 1142 King Stephen's rival the Empress Maud raised Aubrey III to a newly created earldom of Oxford and it is thought that the keep was then constructed to mark his new rank. In 1216 the castle was besieged and taken by King John from Robert, 3rd Earl, and in 1217 it was captured by Prince Louis of France. Robert, 9th Earl was a favourite of Richard II and was created by him Duke of Ireland. However he was unpopular with the other nobles and after he publicly took up a mistress and abandoned his wife Philippa, niece of the Duke of Gloucester, he was driven into exile and his lands, titles and offices confiscated. His uncle Aubrey eventually recovered the earldom but not the hereditary office of Great chamberlain.

Shortly after Edward IV came to the throne, John, 12th Earl and his son Aubrey were arrested at Hedingham because of their strong Lancastrian leanings and taken to the Tower of London for execution. A younger son John, 13th Earl, escaped the mistaken slaughter of his men at the battle of Barnet in 1471 by their allies owing to confusion between the de Vere star badge and the Yorkist sun badge. After several years of exile the earl returned with Henry Tudor and was showered with honours after their victory at Bosworth in 1485, being the first person to be made a Knight of the Garter by Henry. The king later rather ungraciously showed his thanks for hospitality after a stay at Hedingham when he fined the earl 15,000 marks for having a greater number of liveried retainers than was allowed by law. There was another royal visit in 1561, when Queen Elizabeth was the guest of John, 16th Earl at Hedingham for five days. Henry, 18th Earl was the lest of this line to reside at Hedingham, which passed to Elizabeth Trentham on his death in 1625. The 19th Earl was born at the castle but lived elsewhere and the male line came to an end with the death of his son Aubrey, 20th Earl, in his house in Downing Street, London, in 1703.

In 1713 the castle was sold to Sir William Ashurst, a former Lord Mayor of London. He died in 1719, the year that work was completed on a fine new house in the outer bailey. His sons were all short-lived and the castle passed to his daughter Elizabeth, who married Sir Henry Hoghton, of Hoghton Tower in Lancashire. Their daughter married Lewis Majendie. In the late 20th century the castle passed to Thomas Lindsay, both of whose parents were de Vere descendants.

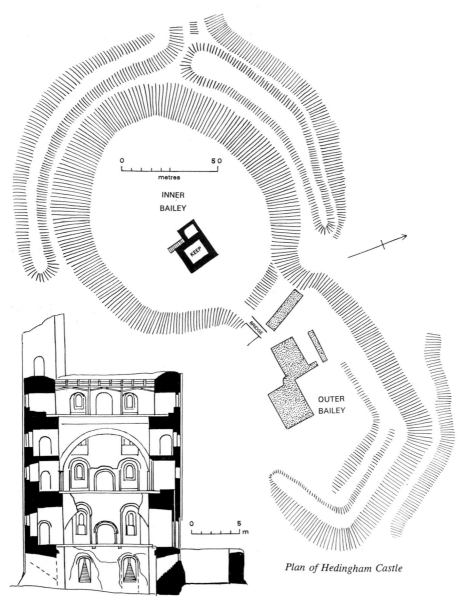

INNER BAILEY

KEEP

BRIDGE

OUTER BAILEY

0 — 50 metres

0 — 5 m

*Plan of Hedingham Castle*

*Hedingham: keep section*

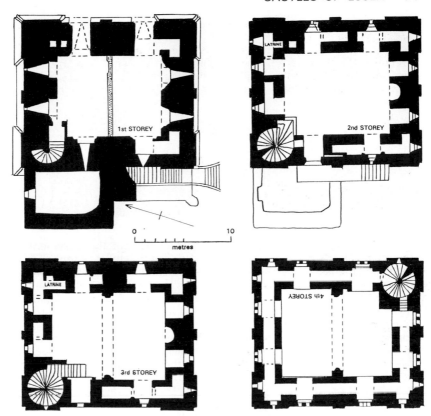

*Plans of the keep at Hedingham*

A natural hillock has been scarped into an oval inner bailey 105m by 85m with an outer bank beyond the formidable ditch on the west and north sides, and to the east there is an outer bailey of similar size with a rampart and an equally deep ditch. The 18th century house lies on the west side of the outer bailey. The inner bailey is assumed to have had a curtain wall but nothing remains of it, nor of any other buildings than the keep, although a hall raised over a vaulted basement is known to have stood SW of the keep. Associated with it were a bakehouse, kitchen and pantries, whilst a chapel is also mentioned in a survey of 1592. Several foundations of both brick and stone were found by excavation in 1868 but are no longer visible. There is, however, a fine brick bridge leading over the ditch into the inner bailey. This was built in 1496 by the 13th Earl, who is known to have added several buildings, including a large red brick tower on the west side of the inner bailey.

The keep measures 17.5m by 15.5m over ashlar-faced walls 3.3m thick above the battered plinth, from which rise pairs of wide pilaster buttresses at the corners and thinner ones in the middle of each side. The building is about 24m high to the wall-walk, the parapet of which is missing, and turrets at the NW and SE corners rise another 6m. It is assumed that there were once turrets at the other corners. The missing turrets and the parapet were probably removed in the 17th century since illustrations of the 1720s and 30s show the castle in the same state as it is now.

*The bridge at Hedingham*

The keep has external openings at five levels, but the basement was a dark storeroom and there were originally only two rooms above, a reception room and a grand court room. The topmost openings were chevron-decorated dummies originally having a pyramidal roof behind them and this level probably only became a habitable space in the 15th century. Marks of the original roof and the sloping gutter onto which it drained can still be seen inside. The fourth level was not a storey in its own right but was a gallery with two-light windows allowing extra light into the court room which is spanned at gallery level by a fine roll-moulded arch. Originally there was a similar arch spanning the reception hall, which has the entrance doorway on its west side close to the spiral staircase in the NW corner. This doorway has nook-shafts with scalloped capitals and chevrons on the arch. It also has a groove for a portcullis, a rare feature in a Norman keep. The doorway may originally have been reached by a wooden stair at right-angles to the wall but before long a stair was erected beside the west wall up to a low forebuilding added outside the doorway. Only the stump of this remains, in a very defaced condition, but the mark of its roof can be seen on the wall above. The reception room and court room both have latrines in the NE corner, a fireplace in the south wall, and two window embrasures on each side. The chambers opening off these embrasures were quite small, only suitable for storage, so it does not appear that the keep contained any sleeping accommodation. Thus it acted as a citadel and status symbol, but not as a residence, for the earls of Oxford must have had their bed-chambers elsewhere. The holes knocked through the east wall of the keep at ground level were made in the early 18th century. The existing floors and roof of the keep are replacements after a fire c1920.

# HOCKLEY MOTTE   TQ 840938

The motte known as Plumberow Mount is thought to have been adapted from a burial mound, Roman and Saxon artifacts having been found in an excavation in 1914.

# MAGDALEN LAVER MOTTE   TL 516084

This motte has a wet moat.

# MOUNT BURES MOTTE   TL 904326

This 14m high motte of the Sackville family has an accompanying village enclosure.

## NETHER HALL    TL 397083

This was a late 15th century moated mansion of brick. One of the two polygonal towers flanking the gateway stands three storeys high but the other has collapsed. Parts of the rooms adjoining the gatehouse also still stand high but the rest has gone.

## ONGAR CASTLE    TL 554032    V

The totally overgrown motte rises 14m above a water-filled moat which completely surrounds it, and there is no access bridge. The top is said to have slight traces of a former shell keep. There were two oval baileys, one on each side, and communication between them could only have been possible via the keep, an inconvenient arrangement. Both still have sections of water in their ditches and the west bailey, which is 130m long by 50m wide, has a rampart and traces of a former curtain wall. The town (now called Chipping Ongar) on this side was also enclosed by a rampart and ditch but the only remnants of it are a section round the NE quarter, next to the castle, and a pond SE of the parish church. The castle of "Angra" is mentioned in 1156 but is assumed to date from the late 11th century.

## ORSETT CASTLE    TQ 641823

This site consists of a round platform or ringwork 58m by 52 with a rectangular bailey 60m by 30m to the NE. There is an outer platform on the east and the outer ditch of this, plus the ditches on the west side still contain some water. On the south side the ditches have been filled in.

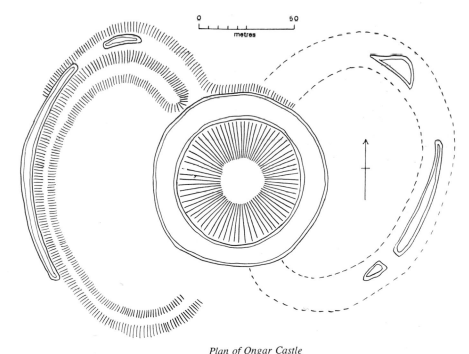

*Plan of Ongar Castle*

## PLESHEY CASTLE    TL 665145    V

This castle is assumed to have been built by the first Geoffrey de Mandeville, who died c1100. His grandson was created Earl of Essex by King Stephen in 1140 but later betrayed the king and ran amok throughout Essex and Cambridgeshire. The first mention of the castle is when King Stephen persuaded Geoffrey de Mandeville's garrison to yield it up in 1143. The third Geoffrey de Mandeville regained the earldom in 1156, but in 1158 Henry II had his castles of Pleshey and Saffron Walden dismantled. Earl Geoffrey's brother William was allowed to refortify the site, probably some time during the 1170s. King John besieged the castle in 1215, and in 1216 it was surrendered to Prince Louis of France. The castle passed to the Bohuns, Earls of Hereford. During Richard II's reign Pleshey was held by his uncle Thomas of Woodstock, Duke of Gloucester who was eventually ambushed by the Duke of Exeter, taken off to Calais on the king's orders, and later strangled. In 1629 Robert Clarke demolished most of the buildings for materials to erect a nearby house called The Lodge, later sold to Sir William Joliffe, whose monument lies in the church.

A late medieval brick bridge leading across the ditch up to the motte is all that remains other than the very impressive earthworks. The motte is 15m high and once bore a rectangular building with angle turrets set on a thin foundation with buttressing. The rampart of the kidney-shaped bailey to the south rises 12m above a ditch which is still full of water. Originally the bailey entrance was probably on the NE where there is an island in the ditch, a position allowing it to be commanded by the motte. A more modest ditch also surrounded the village on the north, and it seems there may have been another bailey on that side. Excavations have shown evidence of late 12th century timber buildings erected against the timber revetted bailey rampart, and incorporating bricks. Footings of a chapel of c1300 with 15th century alterations were also revealed. Two small round foundations of the late 12th or 13th century were found below the chapel.

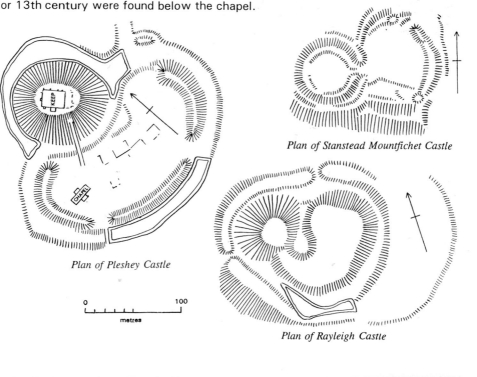

Plan of Stanstead Mountfichet Castle

Plan of Pleshey Castle

Plan of Rayleigh Castle

0                    100
metres

*Pleshey Castle*

## PURLEIGH MOTTE    TL 841017

This is a small motte with a counterscarp bank beyond its ditch.

## RAYLEIGH CASTLE    TQ 805909    F

Domesday Book in 1086 says "in this manor Suene has made his castle", Suene being the son of Robert Fitz Wymarc, who came to England in 1042 with Edward the Confessor. The castle reverted to the Crown in 1163 after Henry de Essex was accused of cowardice during a battle in Wales in 1157 and then defeated in a judicial combat. Henry II's pipe rolls record expenditure on it in 1172 and 1183. There is no mention of the castle in the grant of the castle to Hubert de Burgh in 1215 by King John and it may have recently been abandoned or destroyed. The castle had an inner bailey defended by a deep ditch towards the east, where there was an outer bailey. At the SW the bailey narrowed and swept round as a causeway rising up onto the motte summit, which is 25m across. There is a counterscarp bank beyond the motte ditch. Excavations showed that the motte was at least part stone revetted but no sign was found of a keep on the summit, although traces of a former ditch across the causeway were revealed. In the bailey several rough sloping floors were uncovered plus traces of palisades and a section of the 2.7m thick foundation of a curtain wall which is known to have been destroyed to its base by the 1390s. There was evidence of a square turret at the NE corner. The site is now a public park.

## RICKLING HALL    TL 499302

Close to a 6m high motte lies a moated brick mansion of c1500. The hall in the east part of the south range has gone and the kitchen and service rooms in the west part of than range have become a barn, but the other ranges survive with several original windows, but considerably altered inside. The gateway lies in the north range.

## SAFFRON  WALDEN  CASTLE    TL 540397    F

The Bury Hill east of the church was the bailey of Walden Castle, with a natural slope on the south side. Traces of a bailey curtain wall have been found. At the east end of the site is the defaced stump of a tower keep 19m square over walls up to 3.6m thick still standing about 8m high. A staircase against the west side led up to a forebuilding and entrance at the NW corner at second storey level. From there a spiral stair in the SE corner led down to the basement and up to at least one more storey. The basement had a pier in the middle to help carry the next floor. This level had access to a well shaft in the NE corner and had two recesses in the west wall, which was strengthened there by the stair outside, and in the western part of each of the north and south walls.

The keep was probably begun by Geoffrey de Mandeville after he was created Earl of Essex by King Stephen in 1140, although the castle was confiscated two years later by the king before such a huge building project could have been completed. The site was later repossessed by Geoffrey's son, another Geoffrey, only to be destroyed by Henry II in 1158. Waldon eventually passed by marriage to the Bohun earls of Hereford. In 1347 Humphrey de Bohun obtained a licence to crenellate his house at Walden, which presumably lay in the castle bailey. Whether the keep was then in use, or indeed if it was ever completed, is uncertain. The estate later became part of the Duchy of Lancaster. Lord Chancellor Audley obtained Walden from Henry VIII and after being created Earl of Suffolk in 1603 his grandson Thomas Howard began the splendid mansion of Audley End on the site of Audley Abbey SW of the town.

## ST  OSYTH'S  CASTLE

In 1543 Henry VIII had a coastal artillery fort erected here from the materials of the recently demolished priory. Nothing remains of it.

## STANSTEAD  MOUNTFICHET  CASTLE    TL 516250    O

East of the church is a ringwork 50m in diameter with a surrounding ditch which has been obliterated by gardens on the west. To the east is a bailey about 70m across with a rampart on the north and east, whilst there is a steep natural slope on the south. On the south side of the ringwork is one short low section of walling. It lies at right-angles to the presumed line of a curtain wall so can only have formed part of a tower or some other projection. In 1984-6 the site was provided with a fresh set of palisades and timber buildings as a tourist attraction with costumed dummies to demonstrate the nature of timber-built castles and life within them. The internal buildings look convincing and the animals running around give a good idea of the atmosphere of an 11th century castle but the palisade scarcely seems adequate as a defensive perimeter for a site which is not naturally very strong. The south side (where the ground does slope away quite steeply) seems an unlikely location for a siege tower ever to have been employed for an assault since such a tower could only ever have been pushed forward (by manpower) across fairly level ground.

The castle is assumed to have been built in the late 11th century by Robert Gernon. His son William adopted the name de Montfichet, so this was evidently the principal seat of his barony. His grandson Richard was keeper of the royal forests of Essex and it was perhaps he who provided the ringwork with a stone curtain wall. He died in 1203 leaving a son Richard who on attaining his majority joined the revolt against King John, who is said to have destroyed the castle. Richard later regained the royal favour under Henry III and lived until 1258, when his estates were divided amongst his sisters, but the castle site does not seem to have been reoccupied.

*Stanstead Mountfichet Castle*

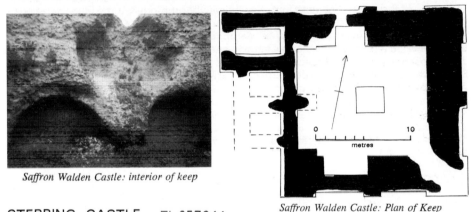

*Saffron Walden Castle: interior of keep*

*Saffron Walden Castle: Plan of Keep*

## STEBBING CASTLE   TL 657244

This is a motte rising 11m from a water-filled ditch to a summit 15m by 10m. There are slight traces of a bailey.

## THORNDON HALL   TL 618918

The existing hall was begun in 1764 by James Paine for Lord Petre. Excavations on the site of the old hall nearby have revealed three periods of construction from 1414 to 1570-90. The hall had a large tower on one side and was later given a semi-circular bastion.

## TILBURY FORTS   TQ   & 651752

The 19th century Coalhouse fort stands on the site of the D-shaped artillery fort of East Tilbury built by Henry VIII in 1539. A similar fort at West Tilbury became part of the riverside defences of the new fort built there by Charles II in the 1670s, but was swept away be rebuilding in the 1860s.

## WILLINGDALE CASTLE   TL 600082

There are slight remains of what seems to have been a motte and bailey site.

# GAZETTEER OF CASTLES IN NORFOLK

## BACONSTHORPE CASTLE    TG 111382    F

A house called Wood Hall originally stood on or near this site and half of the manor which it served was purchased by William Heydon in the early 15th century. His son John acquired the other half and probably began work on the present building, which was then known as Baconsthorpe Hall, in the 1450s. From the Paston Letters it is clear that this lawyer was noted for his duplicity and extortions. Somehow he managed to survive the executions of his original patron the Duke of Suffolk in 1450 and his fellow "extortioner" Tuddenham in the 1460s. In 1451 his enemies tried to interdict him for "riding against the statute". His son Sir Henry built a house at West Wickham in Kent during the 1470s and after succeeding to Baconsthorpe in 1480 substantially enlarged the hall. His son Sir John preferred to reside at Saxlingham and it was he who erected the long building on the east side of the court at Baconsthorpe for the processing of wool from his huge flocks. Despite the use of the place as more of a factory than a residence, the next lord, Sir Christopher added the outer court with its gatehouse. He died in debt in 1579 and his son Sir William was obliged to sell some of the lands. The next lord, Sir Christopher remodelled the inner gatehouse and apartments c1600. His wife's arms were the last of a series that formerly adorned the windows of the inner gatehouse. Sir Christopher's son became Lieutenant-General of Ordnance to Charles I and had his estates taken by Parliament. To pay off his debts after buying them back he demolished the domestic buildings of Baconsthorpe Hall for the value of their materials. The estate was sold to a London merchant in the late 17th century but soon passed to Zurishaddai Lang, a doctor who lived in a house created from the outer gatehouse. This part of the building remained inhabited until its western turret collapsed in 1920. The estate was acquired by John Thruston Mott of Barningham Hall in 1801 and in 1940 the ruin was placed in state care by Charles Mott-Radclyffe. It is now maintained by English Heritage.

*Baconsthorpe Castle*

*Baconsthorpe Castle*

A moat extending from a lake to the east encloses a platform roughly 60m square, although it is slightly bowed on the north side. The original mid 15th century building comprised a court about 33m square set in the SW corner of the platform, bounded by a wall 1.2m thick and having a substantial rectangular gatehouse at the SE corner and turrets 4m square containing small rooms at the SW and NW corners, the latter turret having one keyhole-shaped gunport looking south. The curtain is very ruinous but still rises about 4m above the moat. It is assumed that the great hall lay on the north side but here and on the east all traces of the curtain wall and any buildings within it have vanished. A well marks the likely site of the NE corner tower. In the remodelling of the 1480s and 90s two D-shaped turrets containing latrine rooms serving the main apartments were added to the west side, and rest of the platform was enclosed by a wall 0.9m thick, too thin to support a wall-walk. This wall is pierced by several loops and has a round turret 3.8m in diameter at the NW corner, a tower 6m square at the NE corner, and a tower about 4m square in the middle of the north side. On the east side of the court another rectangular tower adjoins the north end of the mid 16th century building used for wool processing which presumably remained in use after the domestic buildings were dismantled. Shearing was probably done in the lower storey whilst weavers worked in the level above.

*The gatehouse at Baconsthorpe*

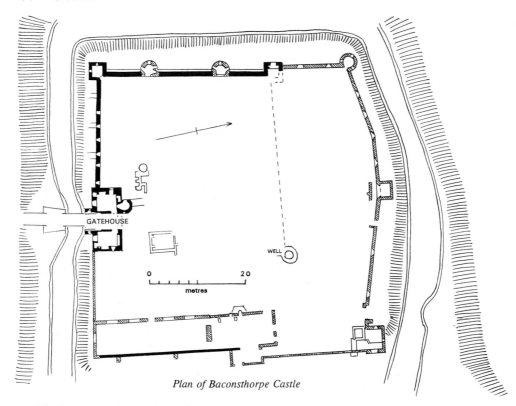

*Plan of Baconsthorpe Castle*

The inner gatehouse is an impressive three storey building faced with knapped flints. It seems to have been a slightly later addition, probably of the 1460s. The passage was vaulted and flanked by comfortable vaulted rooms with fireplaces and latrines probably for the steward and porter. Projecting in front is a two storey porch with loops flanking the moat. The upper rooms were reached by a stair turret on the west side of the inner arch and formed a suite of apartments suitable for the lord and his family, although by the 1490s they had probably moved to more spacious accommodation on the west side of the court. These upper rooms had windows of two and three four-centred lights with hood-moulds. The top room of the porch seems to have been a private chapel with its east window set high enough to allow an altar and reredos below it. NW of the gatehouse is a well and there was evidently a kitchen and other service buildings in this locality.

The outer gatehouse is of similar size to the inner one but is of a generally more domestic nature. Set in the middle of each of the east and west ends were turrets with octagonal superstructures rising from square bases. The passage was flanked by lodges and had a fine chamber above and there was a third storey in the roof. A three storey porch was built on the south side c1700 but this was removed about a hundred years later. On either side are traces of later wings. The outer court never formed a defensive enclosure and was not moated.

## BURGH MOTTE    TG 213261

There is a large but low motte with a water-filled ditch at Hall Farm.

## CAISTER CASTLE    TG 504123    O

Caister was begun early in 1433 by Sir John Fastolf, a renowned soldier who paid for the work out of the proceeds of his part in the wars with France under Henry V and Henry VI. Particularly profitable was his capture of the Duke of Alencon at Verneuil and four years service as Governor of Normandy. The outer court lay on the site of an older house which was plundered during the Peasant's Revolt of 1381 and which was cleared away in 1432. Part of the building accounts survive and record such interesting details as wages being withheld from workmen after a section of wall collapsed into the moat because it was given inadequate foundations. As early as 1434 the windows were being glazed and plastering and roofing operations were under way in 1435, although the castle was not finally completed until 1448, the total cost probably being about £6,000. Sir John purchased Blicking Hall not far away in 1431 and probably lived there until the new castle was habitable.

When Sir John Fastolf died in 1459 Caister passed to John Paston. The Pastons tenure of Caister was contested by several others, including John Mowbray, Duke of Norfolk. The difficult situation is described in the famous Paston Letters between John's son John who was away fighting the French and the rest of the family shut up in the castle. In 1469 the duke besieged the castle with an army said to be 3,000 strong. The garrison of 28 were short of munitions and after five weeks they were forced to surrender, John's widow Margaret and her younger children being allowed to leave. Although the castle is said in the Paston Letters to have been "sore broken with guns of the other party", the siege seems to have been a bloodless blockade except for an incident in which two of the Paston retainers, Pamping and Broon, shot "off a gun at Caister which slew two men". The Duke of Norfolk paid for the victims' widows to pursue the retainers in court afterwards. The younger John Paston managed to regain the castle upon the Duke's death in 1475, and Edward IV eventually confirmed him in possession after a payment of 100 marks. The Pastons then lived at Caister until in 1599 Erasmus Paston transferred to the new mansion of Oxnead Hall, which his father had erected, and was then considered more comfortable.

*Caister Castle*

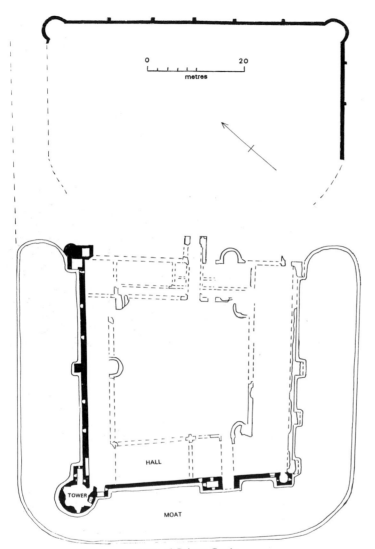

*Plan of Caister Castle*

Caister Castle was one of the earliest major buildings in England to be constructed of brick, although all the dressings are of stone. It consisted of an inner court 42m by 45m with an outer court 60m by 35m to the NE, both parts being surrounded by a water filled moat which was widest (12m) around the inner court and came up right to the foot of the walls. The outer court was entered on its NW side, where the wall is now missing. Towards the NE and SE it has a wall 0.8m thick with a few buttresses and open-backed round bastions of shallow projection at the north and east corners. There are arrow loops in these bastions and since the inner court is furnished with gunloops it is possible that the outer walls of this court were older work. An old plan shows ranges on the NW, NE and SE sides of this court.

*Caister Castle*

The inner court had a wall just 0.8m thick, except for on the NW, where it is 1.2m thick. In order to carry a wall-walk and parapet a greater width was required and the SW wall has brick corbelling for a machicolated parapet. On the NE side, where there was a projecting gatehouse 5m wide, very little of the wall survives, and its inner face is missing on the SE. There were ranges of apartments on all four sides, with the hall being on the SW, with a postern gate south of it in a protecting tower. Little remains of what is said to have been thirty rooms in the inner court except fragments of the footings of their inner walls and what remains of their windows in the outer walls. At each corner were a pair of square turrets containing latrines. At the north corner the angle between the turrets was filled by a small round turret, whilst at the west corner the angle is filled by a most impressive round tower only 7.5m across externally but rising 27m above the moat. The tower has remains of a projecting parapet carried on brick arches and its upper rooms were reached by a spiral stair in a polygonal turret on the SE side which rises still higher. In all there are six storeys of polygonal rooms, all with fireplaces except the topmost, which was probably a muniment room. These may have provided bedrooms for the lord and his family, whose private chambers extended from the west corner of the court (where there was a chapel) towards the north corner. Sir John Fastolfe's own suite of rooms is said to have included a bath, a very unusual feature in the 15th century.

The postern gateway faced towards what appears to have been a third court where there is another round tower 8m in diameter and 10.5m high and a building known as the Barge House straddling a projecting arm of the moat. Originally there was a connection from here to the River Bure, allowing direct access to the castle from the sea. This block and another wing making an L-shaped building was remodelled in the 18th century and remains occupied as the present hall.

## CASTLE ACRE    TF 819151    F

Castle Acre was founded by William de Warenne, who was created Earl of Surrey in 1088 by William II shortly before his death from wounds received at the siege of Pevensey Castle. The castle chapel is mentioned in connection with the founding of the Cluniac priory at Lewes by William and his wife Gundrada, who is known to have died in childbirth at Castle Acre in 1085. Their son William, 2nd Earl, is assumed to have founded the Cluniac Priory not far west of the castle at Acre. After the 3rd Earl was killed in Syria in 1148 whilst on crusade his estates went to his daughter Isabel, who married firstly King Stephen's younger son William of Blois, who died in 1159, and in 1163 she secondly married Henry II's illegitimate half-brother Hamelin. Their son William de Warenne, 6th Earl of Surrey, entertained Henry III at Castle Acre on several occasions when he came on pilgrimage to Walsingham, and John, 7th Earl, likewise entertained Edward I several times at the castle in the 1290s, although his military duties meant that he can not have spent much time in Norfolk. It was he who conducted the siege of Caerlaverock Castle in southern Scotland in 1300, an event commemorated by a famous poem. His grandson John was the last of the Warenne Earls of Surrey. In 1316 he was excommunicated for openly maintaining at Castle Acre a mistress, Matilda de Nerford, his marriage having broken down, and there being no legitimate heir, although he had several illegitimate children. That same year he made over Castle Acre to Aymer de Valence, Earl of Pembroke, probably as an inducement for Pembroke's support for his application to the pope for a divorce.

The 7th Earl eventually got Castle Acre back and on his death in 1374 it passed to his nephew Richard Fitz-Alan, Earl of Arundel. A survey of the castle made after he was executed by Richard II for treason in 1397 gives its value as nil, and after many years of absentee lords it was probably then derelict. In 1558 the 4th Duke of Norfolk sold the property to Sir Thomas Gresham. It was later sold to Sir Thomas Cecil, and then in 1615 the castle and priory site were purchased by Sir Edward Coke. He is recorded as carrying out some repairs to the ruined castle. In 1971 his descendant the Earl of Leicester placed it in state care, and it is now looked after by English Heritage.

*Castle Acre*

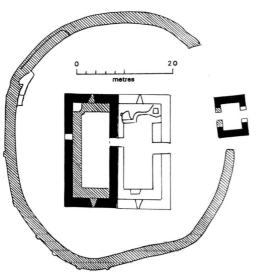

*Plan of upper ward at Castle Acre*

*Town gate at Castle Acre*

Excavations in the 1970s have revealed the interesting architectural development of the upper ward. In c1070-85 this area was given a modest rampart, ditch and palisade around a stone house 24m square over walls 1.5m thick, entered at ground level on the south side, and containing on the upper storey a hall on the south side and a private chamber on the north side of a central spine wall running from east to west. It seems that more unsettled times after King Stephen's disputed accession in 1135 prompted the raising of the surrounding rampart with a curtain wall around a court 48m across and a rectangular gatehouse. The walls of the house were then thickened internally to 3m so that the building could be substantially heightened to form a keep. Whilst the work was in progress there was a another change of plan. The northern section of the curtain wall, which was the most vulnerable to attack as it faced higher ground, was buried in a raising of the rampart and a new wall built at a higher level round this section with timber buildings backed against it. At the same time the southern part of the original house was demolished and the keep built not as a square as intended but as a rectangle with the old spine wall thickened on the south side to make this feasible and the floor level raised nearly 2m. A doorway through the spine wall seems to have been kept to provide a direct access into the basement, whilst a new upper doorway probably further east gave access to the upper storeys. There is a well within the wall-thickness at the NE corner, the shaft being carried up to hall level without access to the water from the basement. Only the lower parts of this keep which were buried in the rampart now survive. It may not have been completed as high as intended, for the work was probably not finished before the 3rd Earl went off on crusade in 1147. Much of the curtain wall still stands to wall-walk level, especially on the west and north, where it has pilaster buttresses facing the field. An opening on the north next to former stairs to the wall-walk led to a tower or latrine. The stepping down of the wall-walk and parapet onto the lower southern section of wall produced a rather odd-looking enclosure. Only foundations exist of the inner gatehouse. It originally had a wide passageway but the level of the road through it was later raised and the inner arch then narrowed.

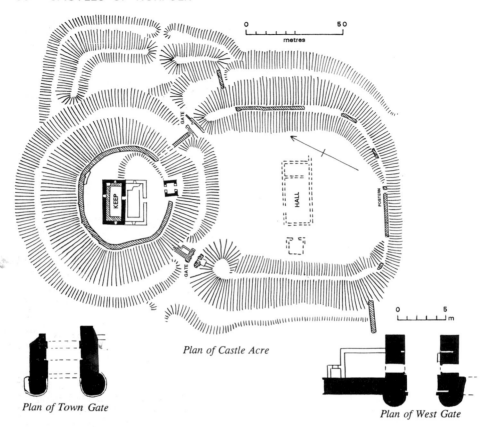

*Plan of Castle Acre*

*Plan of Town Gate*

*Plan of West Gate*

A new wooden bridge connects the upper ward with the lower ward, which is roughly 85m square and extends down the slope to the River Nar. Many centuries ago the river is thought to have been navigable up this far, where it was crossed by the Peddars Way over a ford. The lower ward has high ramparts on the east and west but on the south the river was evidently considered enough protection. On this side is a section of mid to late 12th century curtain wall 20m long still surviving, and footings of other parts can be seen on the ramparts. There was a postern leading to a quay on the south and there are ruined gatehouses on the NE and NW, both of them next to the upper ward ditch. Both were rectangular towers of c1200, that on the west having two small round turrets facing towards the town and a guard-room on the north side, whilst the passage was closed by a portcullis. The town itself has a ditch and has a rather better preserved gateway of the same date and type on the south side of the main street. The NE gate opened towards a smaller outer court or barbican with high ramparts. Evidence of a timber bridge was found here and a new one has been built on its site. A section of walling crossing the lower ward ditch suggests the barbican had a curtain wall. In the middle of the lower ward are traces of 13th century domestic buildings with a central hall running east to west with a detached kitchen near the west end and the parallel building further north could be a chapel. Evidence from the upper ward excavations indicated that from about the time of 3rd Earl of Surrey's death in 1148, that part was used less as a lordly residence and alternative accommodation was developed in the lower ward.

*South end wall of lower ward at Castle Acre*

*The west gatehouse at Castle Acre*

*Base of keep at Castle Acre*

## CASTLE RISING    TF 666246    E

When this castle was founded c1140 by William de Albini its ramparts enclosed the late 11th century parish church, necessitating the construction of a new parish church further north. The gatehouse and keep are assumed to have also been begun c1140, William de Albini having married Henry I's widow Adeliza of Louvain in 1138, succeeded his father in 1139, and then been made Earl of Arundel by King Stephen. During the same period he was building a new castle at Buckenham in Norfolk and rebuilding in stone his wife's seat at Arundel in Sussex. In 1216 King John ordered the sheriff of Norfolk and Suffolk to make timber available for refortifying the 4th Earl of Arundel's castle at Rising. It is likely that the huge earth ramparts of the inner ward then assumed their present size. On the death of Hugh, 6th Earl, in 1243 Castle Rising passed to Roger de Montalt, who was married to Hugh's youngest sister Cecily. The last of the Montalt male line died in 1329 and in 1331, following the terms of an agreement made four years earlier, Castle Rising was handed over to Isabella, the dowager queen of the late Edward II, and formed her chief residence until her death in 1358, although she had other castles at Mold and Hawarden in Flintshire, Hertford, and Mere in Wiltshire. Several times during the 1340s she was visited at Rising by her son Edward III with Queen Philippa.

Castle Rising subsequently passed to Isabella's grandson, Edward the Black Prince. He had the bridge outside the main gate repaired in 1360 and the brick curtain wall may possibly be his work, whilst there is a mention of the "Nyghtyngall Towre" being repaired in 1365. Steps to make sure the castle was adequately garrisoned were taken in the 1380s when a French invasion was feared. On several occasions the castle was alienated by the Crown but in 1402 this was declared illegal and Rising was declared to be in perpetuity part of the Duchy of Cornwall. It was thus held either by the monarch or his eldest son until in 1544 Henry VIII granted the castle to Thomas Howard, Duke of Norfolk in exchange for various lands in Suffolk. Edward IV had the castle garrisoned on his assumption of the throne in 1461. The keep roof was noted as being in a poor condition and not worth repairing in a survey of 1503 in which it was noted the curtain walls "yf they be no amendyd they will fall downe". The curtain wall beside the main gate was rebuilt in 1528 and in 1530 the gates themselves were repaired, whilst the kitchen received attention in 1531. At this time Henry VIII's sister Mary and her husband Charles Brandon, Duke of Suffolk seem to have been in residence. A survey of 1542-3, whilst listing various depredations elsewhere in the castle, especially the "olde greate towre" (keep), refers to a "newe loggyng" with a kitchen, larder-house, chapel and long stable. On the west side of the lower ward a length of wall extends across the ditch to meet up with the former wall or palisade around the town.

*Keep approach steps, Castle Rising*

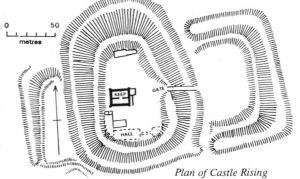

*Plan of Castle Rising*

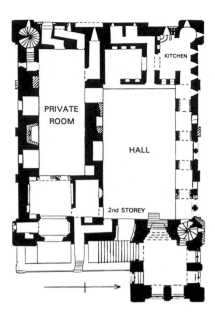

*Gatehouse at Castle Rising*

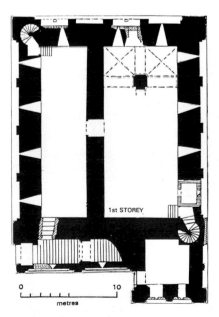

*Castle Rising: Plans of keep*

*Bailey curtain wall at Castle Rising*

A survey made for Queen Elizabeth after the rebellion and execution of the Duke of Norfolk in 1572, declared that repairs would cost £2000 but the materials if the place was dismantled would be worth only £67. In 1693 the Duke of Norfolk sold the ruin to a kinsman Thomas Howard. In 1705 stone was taken from it to repair a sluice on the estate. By the early 19th century the ruin was being regarded as of historical interest and Fulke Greville Howard had the inner ward dug down to its original level and the basement of the keep cleared of debris. The lower parts of the original parish church, long converted to secular use but buried in the 16th century, were revealed. The castle is now maintained by English Heritage.

The castle consists of a pear-shaped inner ward 120m long by 80m wide connected by a bridge on the east side across the deep outer ditch to an outer ward 90m by 60m with its own high rampart and deep ditch, but with north and south entrances next to the ditch of the inner ward. A small second outer court on the west has only a token rampart and no ditch on the south side and this part was either left incomplete or dismantled after access to it was shut off by the raising of the inner ward ramparts which was probably in 1216. These ramparts now rise 18m above the ditch and 9m above the inner ward. The court within them is entered through a square gatehouse with a round arch with a portcullis groove behind it. Not much remains of the upper room, which was reached by a spiral stair in the SW corner, cut off by alterations. In front of the gateway is part of one wall of a barbican. Perched up on the rampart south of the gateway is a leaning fragment of a brick curtain wall with its wall-walk carried over a series of embrasures forming an arcade. The wall seems to have been flanked by several towers and the Buck brothers print of 1738 shows a lofty fragment of a rectangular tower somewhere on the SW side leaning quite dramatically. At the north end is the 11th century church half buried in the later rampart, which blocks original windows surviving in its north wall. It consisted of a nave, central tower and apse, the same layout as the church that succeeded it further north. The position of a Tudor fireplace 3m above the original floor level demonstrated how much silting up had taken place by the 16th century. Between here and the keep is a well. South of the keep are various foundations of buildings. It is known that there were many apartments and service rooms apart from those in the keep. An early 18th century print shows what looks like the east end of a chapel still standing to full height.

outh East Front, The Castle, Castle Rising

*Keep at Castle Rising*

The keep measures 24m by 21m over walls 2.6m thick above a battered plinth and is 15m high to the wall-walk, which now lacks the parapet and corner turrets. At the corners are clasping buttresses and at intervals along the sides are slim pilaster buttresses. These buttresses are of ashlar but the sections of walling between them are rough rubble. The building is of a type now classified as a hall-keep with the 14m long by 7m wide hall set side-by-side with a great chamber above the usual dark basement rooms. Both hall and chamber had windows with heads that were tri-lobed, a very unusual feature for a building of this type. In the hall the lord's table backed onto the large round recess in the south wall probably served as a backdrop to the lord's table, and perheps contained a table for foodstuffs. The recess cannot have been a fireplace since it has no flue and there must have been a central brazier.

The storage basement was intended to be vaulted, the larger room below the hall having three square piers to allow it to be ceiled in eight square bays, but only the two bays below the kitchen and pantry at the west end of the hall and the east end of the south basement below the chapel were actually ever provided with vaults. The passage between the service rooms (and not originally connected to them, although the thin walls are now broken through) leads off to a pair of latrines for which the outer wall on the west side is arched out between the buttresses. The great chamber also has a pair of latrines with an additional urinal in the northern one, which was thus presumably reserved for men. There are spiral stairs in the NE and SW corners of the keep, the SW stair allowing wine to be brought directly up to the great chamber from the cellar below.

At the east end of the great chamber is a chapel with its chancel formed in the thickness of the outer wall. The nave (originally reached only via an ante-chapel from the hall) was arcaded, and vaulted to carry the floor of another room above it reached by a long passage from the NE spiral staircase. Against the east side of the keep is a forebuilding with two flights of steps rising to a square ante-room in a tower projecting 9m from the NE corner. From here another doorway, now blocked by a fireplace, led into the hall. The landing half-way up the steps was closed by a middle doorway, in front of which is a machicolation from a passage above.

The keep at Castle Rising is unusually ornate in its details. The lower doorway of the forebuilding has a roll-moulding above which there is a corbelled frieze of quatrefoils within diamonds. Above is blank arcading of roll-moulded arches and there are chevrons above and billeted bands below. There is also blind arcading with chevrons and billets on the east face of the forebuilding. The angle buttresses have nook-shafts with cushion-capitals near the top of the building at their three outer corners and there are nook-shafts on the pilasters of the forebuilding. More elaborate of all is the portal leading into the hall which has three orders of shafts with roll-moulded arches with bands of chevrons between them.

In the early 14th century parts of the top of the keep were rebuilt and the ante-chamber in the forebuilding was rather crudely vaulted and another room built on top. This suggests that the early Montalts neglected the castle but that it was repaired by the last of them. The mullions and transoms inserted in the ante-room windows probably date from the 16th century when this part of the keep remained in use after the hall and great chamber had become roofless in the 16th century. The vaulted kitchen with its circular fireplace in the NW corner (just as in the keep at Norwich, from which the Rising keep obviously derives a lot of inspiration) and oven and drain also remained in use during this period, being made accessible by cutting through the piers between the window embrasures in the hall north wall to make a passage through from the NE spiral staircase. The fireplace in the great chamber and the postern from the basement below leading onto the foot of the forebuilding stairs are late medieval insertions.

*Town Wall at Great Yarmouth*

*Claxton Castle*

*Claxton Castle*

# CLAXTON CASTLE   TG 334037

Claxton was a courtyard castle with round corner turrets and a wet moat of at least partly circular form. In 1376 Edward III granted William de Kerdeston a licence to complete the crenellating the "mansum" begun by his father under the terms of an earlier licence of 1340, but the parts to which these licences relate may have been swept away during rebuilding by Sir Thomas Gawdy in 1566. The surviving brick wall about 30m long, 1m thick and 6m high looks 15th century work with alterations of probably two periods. A U-shaped turret 3m across near the middle stands 8m high. There are two other turrets at the east end, and parts of a spiral staircase high up. A small isolated masonry fragment stands further east, beyond the farm approach.

# DENTON CASTLE   TM 264895

This small motte and bailey castle with water filled moats is thought to have been erected by the de Albini family in the early 12th century.

# DRAYTON LODGE   TG 187132

In the grounds of a nursing home are ruins of a 15th century building of two storeys with round corner turrets. Sir John Fastolf was lord of Drayton and the lodge has brickwork similar to that of his castle at Caister. It later passed to the Pastons.

# GREAT HAUTBOIS   TG 261203

Nothing now remains of a moated castle for which a licence to crenellate was issued by Edward II in 1313.

*Tower on Town Wall at Great Yarmouth*          *Tower on Town Wall at Great Yarmouth*

# GREAT YARMOUTH    TG 524075

In 1262 Henry III granted six years murage tax to help pay for the construction of a town wall enclosing a strip of land 1.4km long but barely 0.3km wide with the River Yare defending the west side. Rather curiously, the layout feature re-entrant angles at both the NE and SE corners, where impressive towers still remain. In places the walls still stand 7m with the wall-walk and parapet. None of the gates survive but about two thirds of the wall and its towers still stand. The wall-walk was carried on an internal arcade of embrasures with crossloops both in the parapet and below it. The tower at the SE corner is round and measures 5.2m in diameter over walls 1.1m thick but some of the other towers are D-shaped structures of greater size and considerable height. On the east side stood The Mount, a castle or citadel, which was square with corner towers. It is first mentioned in 1399 and was dismantled in 1620.

*The site of Gresham Castle*

## GRESHAM CASTLE   TG 167381

Flint revetment walls up to 3m high and the moat survive of a 40m square courtyard castle with round towers 10m in diameter . Edward II issued a licence for it to be crenellated by Sir Edmund Bacon in 1319. In 1450 it was captured without much effort by Lord Moleyns from John Paston. The site is now heavily overgrown. When the moat was cleaned out in 1846 large timbers of a former drawbridge were revealed together with the keel of a boat and the entrance to a passage.

## HORSFORD CASTLE   TG 205156   F

The very low motte lies on the north side of the side, overlooking a slight slope, whilst the almost ploughed-out bailey lies on the south side. There are said to have been stone buildings and a barbican but nothing remains of them. The castle was built by Water de Cadamo and latter passed to the de Cressy family.

## HUNWORTH RINGWORK   TG 072353

This is a small and very worn down ringwork.

## KING'S LYNN   TF 624198

During the 14th century the north, east, and south sides of the town were surrounded by a wall with a walkway built on an arcade. Fragments of it 1.8m thick and up to 2.5m high survive in Kettlewell Lane, Wyatt Street and The Walks. The south Gate of 1520 still stands, with a stone facade to the field and brick and stone towards the town. It has two pedestrian archways as well as a carriageway and mullioned upper windows and angle turrets and battlements. On the west side of the town the river was considered enough of a barrier. A mound near the SE corner, possibly a motte, is now surmounted by an octagonal brick chapel of c1485.

## MARHAM CASTLE

In 1277 the castle which Sir William Belet was licensed to crenellate by Henry III in 1271 was said to be to the "prejudice and nuisance of the country". According to Blomfield it remained in use for another century before it was given to the Cistercian nuns of nearby Marham Abbey. There are no remains, and the exact site, about 9km west of Swaffham, remains uncertain.

*The keep at Mileham Castle*

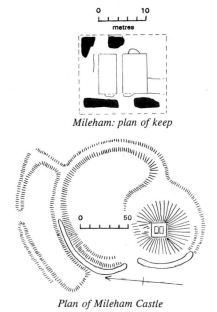

Mileham: plan of keep

Plan of Mileham Castle

Town gateway at King's Lynn

## MIDDLETON TOWERS & MOTTE    TF 661165 & 669175

A motte rises 10m from the 2m deep surrounding ditch to a summit 10m across commanding a considerable view, since it is placed on a hill. The small bailey on the east side is now hardly visible but had a ditch 8m wide and 3m deep. On a low-lying site to the north lies Middleton Towers, a moated mansion built by Lord Scales in the late 15th century. Much of it is now of c1860 and c1900 but there remains a fine brick gatehouse with four polygonal corner turrets and an oriel window on a traceried bracket over the four-centred gateway arch. A second oriel is 19th century.

## MILEHAM CASTLE    TF 916193    F

In 1154 King Stephen gave William de Chesney several manors in Norfolk in exchange for the castle and manor of Mileham. It is thought that Stephen had captured the castle from the Fitz-Alans during the 1140s and given it to the Chesneys but now needed to return it to the Fitz-Alans as part of the terms of the Treaty of Westminster. Documents of the Fitz-Alans relating to Mileham dated 1218 make no mention of the castle and the last mention of it is an inquisition post mortem in 1302, when it was said to be decayed. The castle has a motte with two crescent shaped baileys to the north, the ditches of these being partly water filled. The inner bailey measures about 60m by 110m. A rectangular earthwork on the other side of the road produced pottery of 12th to 13th century date in an excavation in 1968. Hitherto it had been considered much older. Sunk into the motte is the stump of a tower keep 18m by 17m over walls up to 4m thick with the basement divided by a cross-wall.

## MORLEY CASTLE    TG 027176

Within a bend of the Wensum is a strongly moated platform with traces of masonry.

*Keep at New Buckenham*

# NEW BUCKENHAM CASTLE    TM 072926 & 084904

The original seat of the barony of Buckenham given to William de Albini by Henry I was at what subsequently became known as Old Buckenham. This site has ditches, still mostly water filled, around an inner bailey 60m long by 27m wide with a 36m wide outer bailey also 60m long on the south side. The inner bailey is now entered by a causeway on the west and the outer bailey by a causeway on the SW corner, but originally the outer bailey was probably approached from the south and the inner bailey reached through it. The inner bailey rampart rises 6m about the moat and has traces of a former stone curtain wall. In 1138 William's son, another William, married Adeliza of Louvain, widow of Henry I, and was created Earl of Lincoln by King Stephen. It was probably after the Earl of Chester seized Lincoln Castle in 1140 that William was made Earl of Arundel instead, although in the late 1140s he styled himself Earl of Chichester. He began work on the rebuilding of the castles at Arundel and Rising and construction of what became New Buckenham castle 3km to the SE of Old Buckenham is thought to have begun in the same period. The new castle is assumed to have been habitable by 1146 when the old site together with 80 acres of parkland was handed over to Augustinian canons for founding a new priory, a condition of the grant being that the old castle be dismantled, probably for its materials to be reused for the priory buildings.

In its original form the castle at New Buckenham comprised a moated platform about 60m across with a stone gatehouse facing NE towards an outer bailey, and having on the east side, near this gateway, a circular keep. During the troubled reign of King John the 3rd Earl, William, probably strengthened the site by raising the huge earth banks of the inner bailey and it was perhaps then that the site was re-orientated with a new gatehouse and outer ward towards the SW. The lands of the 3rd Earl were ravaged by King John in 1216 when the earl finally deserted the royal cause and his castles were ordered to be destroyed. What happened at Buckenham is uncertain, but there is no evidence that the castle was captured and destroyed. On the death of Hugh de Albini, 5th Earl of Arundel in 1243, Buckenham passed to his sister Matilda, who was married to Sir Robert Tattershall. He is credited with founding New Buckenham parish church, the villagers having until then used the old chapel beside the castle, which still exists, although long converted into a barn.

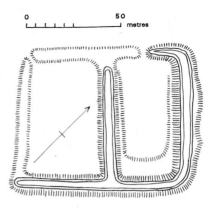

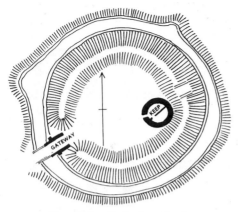

*Plan of New Buckenham Castle*

*Plan of Old Buckenham Castle*

At the start of the war between Henry III and his barons in 1263 Sir Henry Hastings is said to have attacked Buckenham Castle. The reason for the attack was connected with the Mortimers of Attleborough, who must have been in league with the Tattershalls, but the details are unclear. On the death of the 5th Robert Tattershall of Buckenham in 1310, the castle passed to Thomas Cailly. On his death in 1316 Buckenham passed to his sister Margaret's son Adam Clifton, a boy of nine. The last of this line to live at the castle was Margaret, who died in 1447. When her husband Sir Andrew Ogard died in 1454 the castle passed via his sister to Sir John Knyvet. After taking the throne in 1461 Edward IV sent his escheator to seize Buckenham castle. The escheator was able to enter the outer ward but John's wife Alice shouted to him from the top of the inner gate that she would die defending the castle (I.e. the inner ward) and he was obliged to withdraw. The castle remained occupied right up until it was dismantled by Parliament in 1649.

The rampart of the inner ward of New Buckenham castle is an impressive earthwork, rising 12m above the water-filled moat, and now covered with trees on its outer slopes. There is no certain evidence that a curtain wall ever stood upon it. The keep is a most unusual structure. All the other circular keeps in Britain are later than this one is assumed to be and are towers having three or four storeys and a diameter between 10 and 15m. This building is 19.5m in external diameter over walls 3.3m thick, and because of its size has an internal crosswall which supported the next floor but was not continued further up. A door in the crosswall connects the two basement rooms which are all that remain, the walls being 9m high. They are otherwise featureless, and the present entrance was only knocked through in the 18th century. How high the building was intended to be or was ever completed to can only by guessed. A wood cutting of the castle in the church suggests that the keep stood at its present height long before the dismantling of 1649, and that there was an embattled house with two flanking round towers standing in the northern part of the court. A curved footing visible there could be a relic of it. Near the keep is the stump of a later medieval turret on the site of the original east gatehouse. The west gateway has stumps of walls 1.3m thick projecting out towards the moat, where there is a drawbridge pit and remains of a brick barbican probably of late 15th century date. The bridge is an 18th century remodelling of a 13th or 14th century structure. Very little remains of the original eastern bailey but there are traces of a ditch around the village. The later western bailey seems to have had a wet moat.

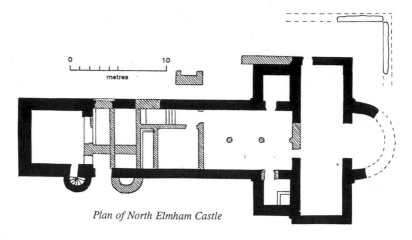

*Plan of North Elmham Castle*

# NORTH ELMHAM CASTLE    TF 988217    F

North Elmham was the site of a Saxon timber cathedral and bishop's palace. Bishop Herfast transferred his seat to Thetford in 1071 as instructed by William I and in 1094 Bishop Herbert de Losinga moved to the present site at Norwich. However, North Elmham remained an important seat of the bishops and in addition to founding a new parish church de Losinga built beside his palace here a large private chapel, until recently considered to be the pre-Conquest cathedral. The nave was aisle-less and ended at the west end in a tower the same width, whilst the east end had a transept with an apse beyond and square turrets were tucked into the corners between the nave and transept west walls. The re-entrant angles were filled with quadrant-shaped fillets of masonry, a very unusual feature. The unusually large west tower is thought to have housed a private oratory for the bishop on an upper storey reached by the spiral stair in a semi-circular stair on the south side which is not a feature usually found in parochial churches of this period, although it is paralleled at the church at South Elmham in Suffolk, almost certainly built by Bishop de Losinga.

*Moat at New Buckenham*

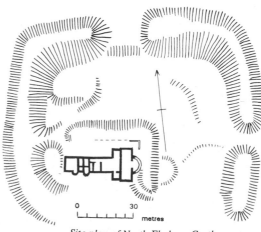

*Site plan of North Elmham Castle*

*North Elmham Castle*

*North Elmham Castle*

In 1387 Bishop Henry Despencer (1370-1406) obtained a licence from Richard II for crenellating his house here which he had converted from de Losinga's chapel. Bishop Despencer was unpopular for his ruthless crushing of the Peasant Revolt and probably felt a need for protection against a similar popular uprising. Externally, apart from the added battlements, the principal changes were the addition of a second half-round turret on the south side so that the original entrance became a gateway with two flanking turrets, the north doorway was blocked up and presumably new upper windows were inserted, now destroyed, since very little of the ruin now stands more than 2.3m high. Internally a hall was created over cellars at the east end of the nave, with the west tower and transept used as chamber-blocks at each end. Part of a straight service stair from the hall west end down to the cellars remains against the north wall. The embattled house thus created lay in the SW corner of a court 95m from east to west by 75m wide surrounded by a 20m wide ditch, well preserved on all sides except on the south where gardens encroach on where it lay. The house was isolated to the north and east by its own more modest ditch. It seems there was an outer court to the east. The building seems to have been allowed to decay by subsequent bishops who were perhaps embarrassed by having possession of a castle converted from a chapel with ditches carved out of a graveyard with scant regard for the burials. The surviving walls were long buried until excavated by Augustus Legge in 1871. The site is now in the custody of English Heritage.

## NORWICH CASTLE    TG 232085    O

William I is assumed to have erected a castle at Norwich in c1067-70, and it is alleged that nearly 100 houses of the thriving Saxon town were removed to make space for it. The castle certainly existed when Ralph Guader, Earl of Norfolk rebelled in 1075, for it was held by his wife Emma (sister of the earl of Hereford) against King William. After a three month siege she surrendered on terms allowing her and the garrison to flee abroad. A garrison more than 300 strong was then installed, suggesting that the rebellion had considerable local support. By 1080 custody of the castle had been given to Roger Bigod, but during the rebellion of 1088 against William II he so oppressed the locality that the locals rose up against him and he was expelled. The castle was of timber until Henry I built the stone keep, probably during the 1120s, when there was a corresponding lull in building work upon the cathedral. In 1136 Hugh Bigod strengthened the castle and refused to surrender it when a false rumour reached him of King Stephen's death, although he handed it over when Stephen came in person to Norwich. Henry II provisioned and garrisoned the castle in 1156, and carried out repairs to the palisades in the 1173, after a recent attack by the rebellious Hugh Bigod, during which the city was sacked. Richard I created Roger Bigod Earl of Norfolk and constable of Norwich Castle in 1189, but the ungrateful earl was soon in rebellion against him in support of Prince John.

King John had the castle repaired in 1204. It was held for him in the struggles of 1215-17 until eventually it was deserted by its commander, Thomas de Burgh, and occupied by Prince Louis of France and his allies. It does not appear that the bailey was walled in stone until the end of Henry III's reign. In later years the castle was occupied by the sheriffs of Norwich and used mainly as a prison. The outer bailey, at least, seems to have been taken over by the townsfolk during the 14th century, and in 1371 the sheriff informed Edward III about Norwich Castle "that no man can dwell in it for the safeguard of the castle nor reside for any other occasion....the stones, timber and lead and other things of the said castle have been broken down, carried and conveyed away". In 1549 Robert Kett, leader of a rebellion which threatened Norwich, until his defeat by the Earl of Warwick at Mousehold Heath, was hanged in the castle. In 1566 the suspected felon Richard Ingham, who refused to speak in court, was slowly crushed to death with great weights placed upon him. The castle was reported to be "decayed" in 1609 and in 1643 it was refortified by Parliament, the defences on the east side being modified to taken cannon. By the 18th century only the keep and the shirehouse still remained. In 1792-3 a new County Gaol was erected on the south side of the keep and blocks of cells were erected within the then derelict shell of the keep. In 1834-9 the forebuilding was removed and the decayed exterior of the keep refaced in Bath stone with the old features faithfully reproduced. In 1887 a new prison was erected on Mousehold Heath and the keep was then gutted and converted into a public museum, a purpose which it still serves.

A natural spur on the western edge of the Saxo-Norman city was shaped into a natural mound isolated by a ditch to the east and south. The mound was large enough to form a bailey with the keep in its SW corner perhaps replacing a small motte. To the south was an outer bailey, probably never provided with a stone curtain wall, although it certainly had a stone gatehouse. Nothing remains of the defences of either bailey except for part of the base of the 13th century inner gatehouse. Excavations have revealed 11th century pottery quite deep down on the site. Nothing appears to be known of the domestic buildings, which seem to have been derelict by the middle of Edward III's reign.

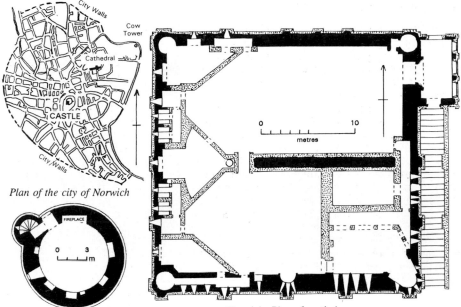

*Plan of the city of Norwich*

*Norwich: Plan of Cow Tower*

*Norwich: Plan of castle keep*

The keep is a most impressive and unusually ornate building, at about 28m square externally and 20m high one of the largest Norman keeps in England. Originally faced with Caen ashlar, it has pilaster buttresses slightly set back from the corners and at intervals along the sides. There are three levels of blind arcading externally into which the windows are set, those of the main rooms being of two tall, narrow lights. Despite the considerable amount of rebuilding both inside and out its original layout is still fairly clear, although internally the present floor level and divisions are quite different. The plan resembles that of the smaller keep at Castle Rising which was evidently built in imitation of the Norwich keep. On the east side steps led first to an intermediate doorway and then up to an ante-room in a forebuilding at the NE corner. The hall doorway from the ante-room has three orders of shafts with lively fighting scenes on the capitals, and beakheads continued round one of the arches. whilst there is a wider outer arch with panels with four-petalled flowers. The hall occupied the north end of the building with at its west end a pantry and a kitchen with its fireplace in the NW corner, with a passage between the two leading off to a pair of latrines. There must have originally been more Norman windows facing north than there are at present. The southern half of the building contained a great chamber (of which the fireplace survives) with a smaller chamber and latrines at the west end whilst to the east was a chapel reached by a passage from the hall. The chapel is thought to have had an aisle on the north side and had an apse in the SE corner to contain the altar. Below all these rooms were dark cellars reached by spiral stairs in the NE and SW corners. The cellars below the chapel are vaulted, and the cellar under the great chamber has a well 30m deep. The top-most tier of windows were for a gallery running round in the thickness of the walls but interrupted at the NW corner by the kitchen fireplace flue. There were no upper rooms, except perhaps over the chapel.

*Norwich Castle: The keep*

*Tower on city wall at Norwich*

Norwich contained a number of semi-defensible buildings apart from the castle and towers of the city walls. The Abbot of Ely is said to have had a fortified house in the city in 1082, i.e. before the cathedral existed. The palace on the north side of the cathedral includes a much altered early 12th century tower-like structure about 14m by 10m externally containing the bishop's chamber over a hall converted by Bishop Salmon into a vaulted kitchen. To the south and east of this building are vaulted undercrofts of the same period. The huge new hall built by Bishop Salmon in 1318 lay to the NE of this. It was unfortified and only the porch remains. The 12th century Jews in Norwich had the wealth to construct stone houses giving them a measure of protection against periodic anti-semitic riots. An example is the Music House of c1175 in King Street which contained a living room and bedroom over rib-vaulted cellars one of which was probably a strongroom for valuables. The stair up to the main living room was contained in a now-destroyed wing on one side.

*Tower on City Wall at Norwich*　　　　　*The Cow Tower at Norwich*

The circuit of city walls at Norwich was 2.75km long, the enclosed areas being on a par with that at London. The city must have had defences roughly along the line of Ber Street by 12th century but the stone walls enclosing an area further west which had already been given a rampart in 1252, leaving the castle then isolated within the city, were begun in the 1290s. They were finally completed by 1343, when they are spoken of as complete and a further grant of murage tax was for improving the ditches. About half the circuit still survives. On either side of the Wensum a kilometre SE of the castle are a pair of ruined towers between which a chain was slung across the river. The north tower is circular and about 6m in diameter, whilst the south tower is D-shaped. From the latter the wall climbs the steep side of Carrow Hill, past one lofty circular halfway up to Black Tower at a corner. This is an impressive building 10m in diameter and 14m high. The section running west of it is arcaded, as is much of the wall. Fragments of the wall with occasional D-shaped towers then sweep round in an arc on the inner or north and east side of Queen's Road, Chapelfield Road (which has a long surviving section), Grapes Hill and Barn Road. One tower is incorporated in the Drill Hall at the junction of Chapelfield Road and Chapelfield North, and another south of here has a polygonal outer face, although it is round inside. The wall then crossed the river and then swept north, fragments appearing on the south side of Bakers Road, Bakers Road, and Bullclose Road. The polygonal corner tower on the north side of Barrack Street has a second storey rib-vault partly remaining, although the back wall is missing at that level. The wall then crossed the river a third time and then followed the south bank of the river out to the Cow Tower, before eventually crossing the river a fourth time and sweeping east. The Cow Tower faces higher ground across the river and is an impressive brick structure of the 1370s with stone dressings. It is 15m high and 11m in diameter with a spiral staircase in a higher turret adjoining the SW-facing entrance. The tower contained three storeys of rooms with cross-shaped shooting slits. There are no signs of a stone or brick wall adjoining it so this section of the defences protected by the river may have been of wood. The Cow Tower is now in the custody of English Heritage. South of the Cow Tower is the Bishop Bridge, the only medieval crossing over the river to remain. Until it was dismantled in 1791 because its weight was making the bridge collapse, there was a gatehouse with four corner turrets perched over the westernmost arch.

*The gatehouse at Oxburgh*

## OXBURGH HALL    TF 743103    O

In 1482 Edward IV licensed Sir Edmund Bedingfield to build walls, towers and battlements at his house here. His grandmother Margaret inherited Oxburgh from her brother Sir Thomas Tuddenham when he was executed for treason on Tower Hill in 1462, his family having held the manor since it passed to them from the de Weylands in 1274. Sir Edmund inherited in 1476 and may have soon begun work on the house for the licence forgives him for any fortifications already made. The house measures roughly 50m square and had four ranges of apartments of brick set within a water-filled moat crossed by a bridge on the north side to a lofty three storey gatehouse with octagonal turrets facing the field. One turret contains small rooms and the other a spiral staircase. Their exterior faces have sunk panels each with three small arches at the top. The gatehouse is essentially a show-piece and the house was not seriously defended, having thin walls with large two-light windows at both upper and lower levels. There do not appear to have been any other towers or turrets originally, although there are a few cross-loops, mainly in the east turret of the gatehouse and in the bartizans corbelled out of its southern corners at parapet level.

Sir Edmund was made a Knight of the Bath by Richard III in 1483, and in 1487 was created a knight banneret by Henry VII. This king visited Oxburgh ten years later, he and Queen Margaret taking the rooms in the gatehouse. Sir Henry Bedingfield, first of nine of this name, was one of the first to support Princess Mary before she became queen in 1553. He was heavily fined as a Catholic by Elizabeth I and the priest's hiding hole was created during her reign. The Bedingfields were Royalists during the Civil War, when the hall was partly damaged by fire. Sir Henry was created a baronet in 1661 by Charles II, his main seat then being at Beckhall, although the damage at Oxburgh was later made good by the 2nd Baronet. In the early 18th century the southern part of the east range was rebuilt by the 3rd Baronet. In the 1770s Sir Richard, 4th Baronet pulled down the medieval hall in the south range, rebuilt the bridge which formerly stood on this side and built new apartments at the SE and SW corners, the latter replacing the medieval kitchen. Sir Henry, 6th Baronet, in 1830 adopted the additional name of Paston, whose heiress he married. It was they who laid out the present arrangement of the room, built the SE corner up as a four storey tower, added the projecting bays and all the existing parapets except those on the gatehouse. The final addition in the late 19th century was a single storey gallery built across the south side. The Bedingfields still live at Oxburgh, but it has been in the care of the National Trust since the 1950s.

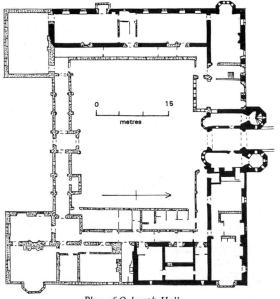

*Plan of Oxburgh Hall*

*Thetford Warren Lodge*

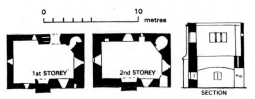

*Plans and section of Thetford Warren Lodge*

## THETFORD CASTLE    TL 875828 & 862831    F

On the east side of the town is a huge motte rising 13m to a summit 24m across. It and a bailey to the east lie within a double rampart and ditch of an Iron Age Fort. Excavations in 1962 showed that the motte top was chalk rubble. Pits in the bailey were found to contain late 11th century to mid 13th century pottery and an outer bailey was discovered on the north side. Buildings on the southern part of the site incorporate diagonally-tooled ashlar blocks. Near the river west of the town is a ringwork which produced Saxo-Norman pottery in an excavation of 1957-8 which showed that it overlay the late Saxon ditch of the town, whose centre then lay on the south bank of the river. Domesday Book in 1086 shows Thetford as shared between the king and Roger Bigod and it is possible they both had castles here at the same time, especially as they are on opposite sides of the river over a kilometre apart. If so the motte would probably be the king's, but was perhaps taken over by Bigod as the stronger of the two about the time when he founded the Cluniac Priory in 1103. Henry II confiscated the castle from Hugh Bigod, Earl of Norfolk in 1157 and he destroyed it as the start of the rebellion of 1173. The site may have remained occupied for a while but it was never refortified.

## THETFORD: WARREN LODGE    TL 839481    F

This two storey building was built c1400 by Thetford Priory supposedly to house their gamekeeper, the rabbit warren here in particular being very productive, but it may have originally served more as a hunting lodge for the prior and his high status guests. The house measures 8.5m by 5.8m over walls 1m thick and is included here mainly because it has an internal machicolation over the entrance on the south side. The nearby SW corner originally had a staircase in a projecting turret. The building is roofed but no longer has an upper floor. Both storeys have fireplaces in a projecting breast and the upper storey also has a latrine.

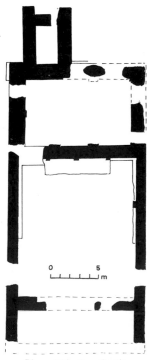

*Motte at Thetford*          *Plan of Weeting Castle*

*Window at Weeting*

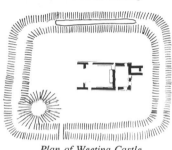

*Plan of Weeting Castle*

*Weeting Castle*

## WEETING CASTLE    TL 777891    F

Within a wet-moated platform 65m by 48m is a ruined 12th century building about 26m long by 15m wide over walls about a metre thick. It contained a hall and chamber over cellars, although there is no sign of a doorway between the two parts at the upper level. The hall seems to have been vaulted, very unusual for an upper floor hall. There was a third storey over the chamber. Projecting from the end wall here is a square wing containing small chambers on the lower two levels. It seems to be of the same date and contains the only windows now surviving, facing west. There seem to have been further rooms at the north end. The ice-house covered with earth in the NW corner of the site has led some writers to think there is a motte.

## WOOD NORTON MOAT    TG 013289

In 1342 Edward III licensed Sir John de Norwich to embattle his houses of Blackworth and Wood Norton in Norfolk, plus Mettingham in Suffolk. Most of his energies seem to have gone into developing Mettingham and there is only a modest moated platform at Wood Norton.

## WORMGAY CASTLE    TF 659117

Wormgay became a barony during William I's reign and the castle was probably founded in that period. It consists of a large but low ringwork and a spacious bailey on the east side.

## WYMONDHAM CASTLE    TG 126203

The priory was founded by William de Albini in 1107 and he may have erected the large low ringwork, now very overgrown, 2km ENE of it at about the same time.

# GAZETTEER OF CASTLES IN SUFFOLK

## BUNGAY CASTLE    TM 337896    F

The first mention of this castle is in 1140 when it was captured by King Stephen from Hugh Bigod, Earl of Norfolk, although Roger Bigod probably founded it before 1100. Earl Hugh later recovered the castle, only for it to be confiscated by Henry II in 1157. It was returned to the earl in 1165 but was captured by the king during the rebellion of 1174 and subsequently demolished. What condition the castle lay in between then and its fortification by Roger Bigod under the terms of a licence granted by Edward I in 1294 is uncertain. On his death in 1306 the castle passed to Thomas of Brotherton, a younger son of Edward I. His daughter Margaret married one of the Mowbrays, and from them in 1483 Bungay passed to the Howards. In 1766 the long-ruined castle was sold to a local builder called Mickleburgh. The mine gallery under the SW corner of the keep seems to be a relic of his attempts to dismantle the walls to provide stone for road repairs, and not a relic of Henry II's siege and destruction of the castle as was once claimed. What remained of the castle later passed to Elizabeth Bonhote, the wife of a local solicitor. She took a liking to the picturesque ruins and had a four storey house for summer use built between the gatehouse towers. By 1817 this too had become ruinous and the town reeve ordered it demolished in 1841. The Duke of Norfolk obtained the site in 1898 and in the 1930s the ruins were excavated under the guidance of Hugh Braun and conserved. Since 1987 the site has been owned and maintained by the Bungay Castle Trust.

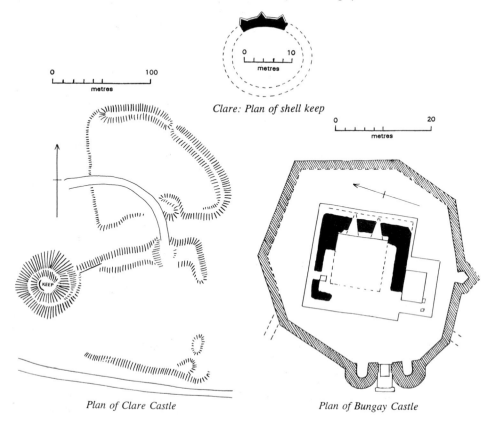

Clare: Plan of shell keep

Plan of Clare Castle

Plan of Bungay Castle

*Gatehouse at Bungay*

The castle and town lie within a long loop of the River Waveney and were thus protected to the east and west by water and marshes. The low motte lay in almost the middle of the rectangle enclosed by the town ditch and rampart, with the inner bailey about 60m wide extending a similar distance out to the west and a larger outer bailey to the south. The latter has now been built over and some of its defences obliterated, but the SW section of its rampart survives. The rectangular keep was almost square at 21m by 22m and had a forebuilding on the south side with steps up towards it from the east. The latrine in the forebuilding basement suggests use of it as a prison. Above the base the walls are missing on the west and elsewhere only stand another 3m high in a very defaced condition with evidence of two loops facing east and another facing north. These must have lighted the storage basement since they seem inadequate for the lighting of a hall, and for this reason it is likely that the two spaces below, lacking any lighting, ventilation or means of access, were simply filled up with earth. A well shaft remains on the north side. This keep is often assumed to have been built between when the castle was returned to Hugh Bigod in 1165 and its capture in 1173, but it could in fact be of the 1140s. How much of this keep still stood and whether it remained in use when a polygonal stone walled court 40m across was later built around it is debateable. The 2m thick wall of this court is now much broken down although the base remains complete all round. It had one flanking tower on the south and was entered from the inner bailey by a gateway with a drawbridge pit flanked by a pair of D-shaped towers. The towers contained small rooms but were without any loops facing the field, which is rather unusual. This work is attributed to the 1290s but seems conservative in design for that period. Little remains of the walls around the inner bailey, but it is known that there were round towers flanking the NW and SW corners and a gatehouse with twin round towers facing SE on the edge of the former ditch between the bailey and keep. This layout recalls that of the bailey at Cambridge as refortified by Edward I in the 1280s.

*Bungay: interior of the keep*

## BURGH  CASTLE    TG 475046    F

The east, south and north walls remain of a Late Roman fort built to protect a small dockyard against Saxon invaders and known as Gariannonum. The walls stand 4.5m high and are 3.3m thick at the base tapering to 1.5m thick at the top and enclose a six-acre space 190m by 100m. The west wall had already collapsed by the late 11th century when an oval motte, removed in 1639, was raised over the fort SW corner (where there was a cemetery of a Saxon monastery) and a rampart was built along the then open west side. The wall was breached for the motte ditch and vertical holes made in it for heavy timbers which held the mound together and supported the timber tower on top of it.

## CLARE  CASTLE    TL 771452    F

This castle was founded in the 1070s by Richard Fitz Gilbert as the centre of his huge Anglian lordship, from which his descendants after c1120 took the surname of de Clare. Subsequently much of their interest lay elsewhere, as they became lords of Glamorgan and eventually built the huge castle of Caerphilly and several others there, as well as having Tonbridge in Kent. The male line ended when the young Gilbert de Clare, Earl of Gloucester was killed in the English defeat at Bannockburn in 1314. The heiress Elizabeth de Burgh frequently visited Clare until her death in 1360. The castle later passed to the Mortimers and from them in the 1430s to Richard, Duke of York. From 1461, when his son became Edward IV, Clare became a property of the Crown.

The castle was tucked into an angle between the River Stour on the south and the Clinton stream on the east. It consisted of a high motte with an inner bailey extending to the east and south of it and a very large outer bailey to the north. The outer bailey contained a priory until this was removed to Stoke-by-Clare in 1124. It has a rampart remaining on the east side. The inner bailey has been mutilated by the intrusion of a former railway and its station, with a former goods-shed now standing isolated in the middle. Station Road enters the inner bailey at a point where the gatehouse stood. Quite a long a high section of curtain wall about 1.4m thick survives west of it, crossing the site of the former motte ditch and beginning to ascend the slope. A spiral path leads up the tree-clad side of the motte to the summit, on which stands the west part of an oval shell keep. The three very unusual triangular buttresses suggest a 13th century date for this.  See plans on page 72.

*Curtain wall at Clare Castle*

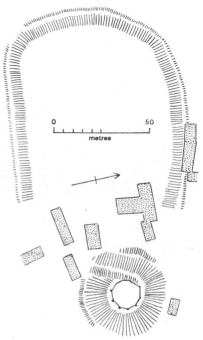

*Plan of Eye Castle*

## COMBS MOTTE    TM 033570

This is a small mound.

## DENHAM CASTLE    TL 747628

A bailey 70m across lies SW of a low motte with a dished top 16m by 20m. The ditch surrounding the site is partly water filled.

## DUNWICH CASTLE

The site of this castle is probably now covered by the sea. It is mentioned in 1217 but there is no mention of it during the attack on the town during the revolt of 1173.

## EYE CASTLE    TM 147737

William Malet built this castle a year or two before being killed during William I's blockade of the Isle of Ely in 1071. The castle is mentioned in Domesday Book in 1086 and about that time Robert Malet founded a Benedictine priory close by. On his death in 1106 Eye reverted to Henry I and was granted to his nephew Stephen of Blois, who became king in 1135. In 1157 the castle was taken from his son William de Blois by Henry II. A reference in 1179 to the repair of buildings damaged "in time of war" suggests a siege during the rebellion of 1173-4. The castle was later held by Henry, Duke of Brabant. There are mentions of the castle in the late 13th century in connection with castle-guard payments but nothing is further known of the building itself, which was probably ruinous by the 14th century, since its later lords had many other residences and rarely used it. Henry III gave Eye to his brother Richard, Earl of Cornwall, whilst in the 14th century it was held by the Ufford Earls of Suffolk and their successors the de la Poles. The polygonal shell keep on the 12m high and rather overgrown mound is a 19th century folly, perhaps on old foundations. The town has now encroached upon the bailey, which lay to the SW. There are traces of what seems to be an old wall ascending the motte from the bailey on the NW. Part of the bailey ditch is visible in Buskshorn Lane.

*Framlingham Castle*

# FRAMLINGHAM CASTLE    TM 287637    E

Roger Bigod held Framlingham at the time of Domesday Book in 1086 as the tenant of Hugh, Earl of Chester, and the earthworks probably existed before he died in 1107. The castle is first mentioned in 1148, when Hugh Bigod, Earl of Norfolk entertained Theobald, Archbishop of Canterbury within it. Henry II confiscated the castle in 1157, returned in 1165, and destroyed it ten years later because of the part that Hugh, then aged about eighty, had played in the rebellion by the kings sons in 1173-4. In 1189 Richard I allowed Richard, 2nd Earl of Norfolk to reoccupy Framlingham and it was then that the curtain walls were erected. Earl Roger entertained King John at Framlingham in 1213, but he later joined the rebellion against him and the castle was besieged and captured by John in 1216. The 4th earl was created Earl Marshall by Henry III in 1246, but this title was lost when the 5th earl, another Roger, refused to serve Edward I in Gascony. After his death in 1306 Framlingham reverted to the Crown, being granted in 1312 by Edward II to his half-brother Thomas de Brotherton, created Earl of Norfolk. His heiress brought the estate to Thomas Mowbray, who in 1397 was created Duke of Norfolk by Richard II, although he was exiled for his part in a private war in 1399. After his son Thomas was executed by Henry IV in 1405 custody of Framlingham was given to Prince Henry. Not until 1425 did Thomas's brother John regain the Dukedom and begin to reside at Framlingham. It was his son John, 4th Duke, who succeeded in 1461, who besieged and captured Caister Castle.

In 1476 the castle passed with an heiress to the first duke's grandson John Howard, who in 1483 was created Duke of Norfolk by Richard III, and died fighting alongside the king at the battle of Bosworth in 1485. His son Thomas was eventually restored to his estates by Henry VII but only regained the dukedom after his decisive victory over James IV of Scotland at Flodden in 1513. The third Duke eventually lost the favour of Henry VIII, being in the Tower of London awaiting execution when the king died in 1547. The new young king, Edward VI, gave Framlingham to his sister Mary and it was here that her supporters rallied to her in 1553 during the few days when the Duke of Northumberland was attempting to put Lady Jane Grey on the throne. Mary gave Framlingham back to the Duke of Norfolk but he never lived there again, and in 1572 his grandson, the 4th Duke was executed by Elizabeth I for treason. The castle was let to tenants and was described in a survey of 1589 as in considerable need of repair. James I restored the castle to the Howard family but in 1635 they sold it to Sir Robert Micham, who in 1636 bequeathed it to Pembroke College, Cambridge, stipulating that the building should be demolished and replaced by a poor-house, although luckily the outer walls were allowed to remain. The poor-house closed in 1837 and in 1913 Pembroke College placed the castle under the guardianship of the Office of Works, whose eventually successors in this role are English Heritage.

The castle consists of a stone walled inner ward 90m by 60m with on the west side a lower court (partly if not wholly stone walled) extending down the slope towards the River Ore, which was dammed to form a lake, whilst around the south and east sides extends a very large outer bailey, at least part of the ditch of which contained water. This outer bailey may be a later addition since it occupies much of the space enclosed by a more feeble outer ditch thought to have been intended to enclose a township. There is a mention of the repair of the palisade around this bailey in 1295. Excavations in 1969-70 showed that there was originally a motte at the north end of what is now the inner ward, but presumably this was levelled as part of the slighting of 1175. Only the timber defences seem to have been destroyed for built into the later curtain wall on the east side of the inner ward is the east wall of a mid 12th century hall block with two original chimneys still remaining. The arrangement of these, one on each of two levels, suggests the unusual layout of a private chamber set above a hall at ground level, with service room at the north end.

*Framlingham Castle*

The circuit of curtain walls around the inner ward at Framlingham is one of the best preserved in Britain. Framlingham and Carisbrooke in the Isle of Wight are the only two places in England where it is possible for the general public to climb up onto an unrestored medieval curtain wall-walk and make a complete circuit around a courtyard of considerable size at that level (this is also true of six 13th century castles in Wales). The wall is 2.3m thick and 12m high to the wall-walk. It is flanked by thirteen rectangular towers which mostly have open gorges towards the court, but at wall-walk level they had timber floors and backs. From the wall-walk, which is reached by a spiral stair in a tower on the west side, wooden ladders gave access to the tower battlements at a higher level. Most of the towers are between 6m and 7m in width externally but one on the west is just 4m wide and one on the east is 12m wide since it enveloped the east end of a mid 12th century chapel at the south end of the old hall. The ghosts of the pilaster buttresses of the chapel east wall can be seen on its inner face. Overall the courtyard shape is ovoid with the towers marking slight angles of the curtains but on the SE the curtain has an almost right angled corner and the 7m square tower there has its potentially very vulnerable outer corner chamfered off. The next tower to the west has mostly collapsed since 1786, the only imperfection in a defensive circuit otherwise little changed during 800 years.

Facing SW is a gatehouse with a portcullis groove in the passageway. The four-centred vault, outer arch and panel of the Howard arms above is early 16th century. Also of that date is the bridge, although the parapets are later, whilst it incorporates the remains of the piers for a late 13th or early 14th century drawbridge. Beyond the ditch once lay a semi-circular barbican probably of 16th century date. The sections of curtain wall east of here are pierced by pairs of loops set in round arches embrasures. Probably in this position were the soldiers' lodgings re-thatched in 1295. A well lies not far from the gatehouse and there were kitchens on the SW side of the court, where large fireplaces can be seen. Fireplaces were later inserted into the northern towers to serve a 16th century lodgings at that end and these have ornate brick chimneys rising above the parapets. The chimneys on the other towers are dummies, except that of the wide tower over the chapel on the east. On the west side of the court is a round-headed postern gate with a draw-bar slot which opened onto an open passage between two high walls extending down the slope to a now-fragmentary rectangular tower containing a prison in its base. Next to the tower was a south facing postern, whilst further east on the north side was the access doorway to the lower ward. The presence of 16th century windows and evidence of a later overall roof suggest the passage was later converted into a gallery. On the north another wall descended the slope to an open-gorged tower with the base of a spiral staircase. A postern from the lower ward to the outside was set between this wall and the north tower of the inner ward. The rest of the circuit of the lower ward only ever had a timber palisade, part of which was renewed in 1295.

A new great hall on the NW side formed part of the work of the 1190s, there being several original window embrasures there in the outer wall. The existing central block here, built to serve the poor-house, is of 1729. The brick southern cross wing is of c1640, whilst the northern cross wing incorporates the east wall of the original solar block, a 16th century chimney breast, and work of other periods. The hall must have been improved at various times, the de Brotherton arms said to have once adorned the entrance being evidence of this. Eventually the castle contained a large number of rooms and there is a record of a range built across the court with chambers over what was described as a "cloister", being demolished in 1700.

# FRECKENHAM CASTLE    TL 667718

A garden now occupies the bailey of a small motte and bailey castle.

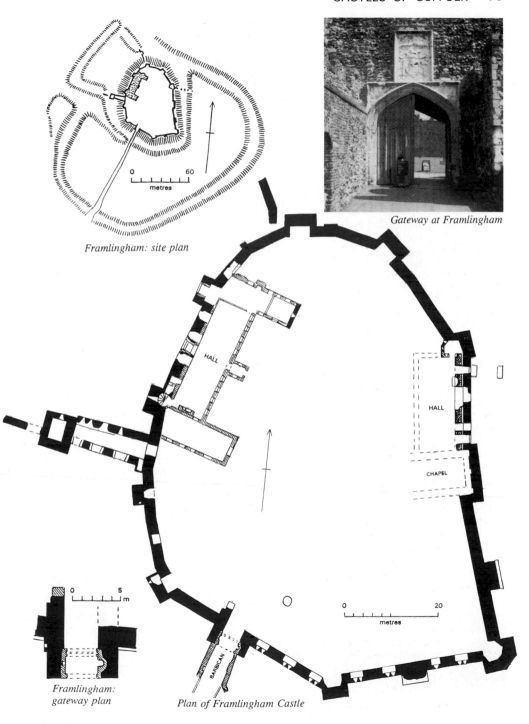

Framlingham: site plan

Gateway at Framlingham

HALL

HALL

CHAPEL

Framlingham:
gateway plan

BARBICAN

Plan of Framlingham Castle

# GREAT ASHFIELD MOTTE    TL 991675

This motte rises 7m from a wet moat to a summit 14m by 9m.

# GROTON MOTTE    TL 963426

The 6m high "Pytches Mount in Groton Park has been dug into at the top.

# HAUGHLEY CASTLE    TM 026624

The fine, if rather overgrown, earthworks are assumed to go back to the time of Hugh de Montfort, noted in Domesday Books as a major landholder in Suffolk. Robert de Montfort was banished by Henry I in 1107 and his sister Alice took the castle to her successive husbands Simon de Moulins and Robert de Vere. King Stephen granted Haughley to Henry de Essex, Lord of Rayleigh but he was disinherited by Henry II in 1163 after being accused of cowardice and defeated in judicial combat. The castle was captured and destroyed by Robert, Earl of Leicester and Hugh Bigod, Earl of Norfolk during the rebellion of 1173 and it does not seem to have been used again. The huge motte rises 24m from the surrounding wet moat to a summit 24m across said to bear traces of a former shell keep. A house lies in the middle of the 90m square bailey to the south with its own rampart and ditch. It is entered from an outer bailey to the west.  See plan on page 5.

# HUNSTON MOTTE    TL 978677

The damaged motte SE of the village has a water-filled ditch.

# ILKETSHALL CASTLE    TM 368880

NE of the village is a motte rising 7m to a summit 20m across. The ditch, sometimes wet, is 2.5m deep. A bailey with its own ditch extends to the south.

# IPSWICH CASTLE

In 1153 King Stephen's castle at Ipswich was captured by Hugh Bigod, Earl of Norfolk. There are no remains either of the castle or of the town walls licensed by Edward III, but footings of a town gate have been traced.

*Little Wenham Hall*

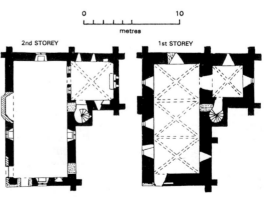

*Little Wenham: Plans*

## LIDGATE CASTLE    TL 721582

The church lies in the south outer enclosure of a platform about 45m square with a ditch 18m wide. There is water in the ditch west of the church and in the outer ditches of a long narrow northern enclosure and a D-shaped one to the east. A castle here existed in King John's reign.

## LINDSEY CASTLE    TL 980442

In the 1140s this castle was held by Adam de Cockfield, a tenant of Bury St Edmunds Abbey, who was given certain outlying manors with a brief to protect them against the hostile lords of the castle of Milden and Offton. John licensed Thomas de Burgh to fortify this site in 1204. It has a low mound 43m across on top lying within an outer court 150m across bisected by a stream which once filled the moats.

## LITTLE WENHAM HALL    TM 082391

This embattled solar block of c1270-80 standing within the middle of a platform enclosed by a wet moat is one of the earliest brick domestic buildings in England. It has a main block 13.5m long from north to south by 7.3m wide which contained a fine private chamber over a basement which is rib-vaulted in brick in three bays, the walls being 1.4m thick lower down but only 0.9m thick above the vault. The basement has a doorway with a drawbar-slot in the south end wall, where a timber framed hall overlapped the corner. The chamber was entered by steps to a doorway, now blocked, at the south end of the west wall. Opposite it is another doorway which originally led to a projecting latrine. The chamber has an original two light window near the middle of each of the four walls, and a wide 16th century fireplace on the west side. The lower part of the projecting stack built up from ground level is original so there was evidently always a fireplace in this position. At the north end of the east side is a square wing containing a vaulted cellar at ground level, a rib-vaulted chapel at hall level, and a bedroom above. This breaks a basic rule of medieval planning that the only thing that should stand above a chapel is another chapel. The chapel has a fine three-light east window with Geometrical tracery with quatrefoils in circles and there is a piscina. The doorway into it from the hall is flanked by two-light openings as in a monastic chapter-house. In the re-entrant angle between the main block and wing is a square turret containing a spiral stair originally linking all the rooms. Both main block and wing have paired-angle buttresses and are embattled with loops in the merlons, whilst the stair turret rises still higher.

The chamber block seems to have been built by either Roger de Holebroke or his kinsman John de Holebroke, who took possession in 1294, both of them ranking as tenants of the Vaux family. The chapel vault boss has a representation of St Petronella, possibly an allusion to John's wife of that name. By 1331 the house had passed to Gilbert de Debenham. His descendant Gilbert de Debenham IV was a noted Yorkist and the hall suffered an attack during the short period of Lancastrian recovery in 1470. His son Gilbert de Debenham V was attainted by Henry VII and was either executed or died in prison in 1500. His sister Dame Elizabeth Brewes recovered the hall the following year. Her great-grandson Sir John Brewes made a few alterations in 1569. That date plus an inscription appears on the chamber block. About this time a new hall was built outside the moat and the old hall was dismantled, leaving the chamber block in splendid isolation, as it is now. In 1695 the Brewes (by then spelt Bruce) family sold Little Wenham to Joseph Thurston, a Colchester barrister. His son William was the last inhabitant of the old chamber block. He sold the estate to Philip Havons in 1765 for £5,500.

*Mettingham Castle*

*Mettingham Castle*

# METTINGHAM CASTLE   TM 360887

In 1342 Edward III licensed Sir John de Norwich to crenellate a castle being built here out of the proceeds of the wars with France. On the death of his grandson Sir John, here in 1373, the castle passed to his cousin Catherine de Brews, a nun at Dartford in Kent. She conveyed the castle to a secular college founded at Raveningham by the first Sir John, and in 1394 the college transferred itself to the castle. After the college was suppressed in 1542 the castle was granted to Sir Anthony Denny.

The castle has a north court 90m by 80m and a slightly larger southern court, both with moats up to 9m wide, although the north and west arms of the moat of the north court have been filled in since 1865. This court, referred to as the "base courte" in a survey made for Sir Nicholas Bacon in 1562, has a curtain wall remaining on the SW and on the north, where there is a lofty gatehouse in the middle. The gatehouse has polygonal turrets on the north corners and stumps of walls of a barbican, the wall-walks of which were reached by doorways from the room over the gateway passage. The curtains contain several openings of rooms built against them. There are no traces of any corner towers but in the middle of the west side is a small square building which stood within the curtain. On the south side of the north court there stood in 1565 a ground floor hall with a two storey chamber block to the west with a buttery, pantry, kitchen, bakery and brewhouse. Isolated within its own moat in the NW corner of the southern court, but reached from the northern court was a citadel possibly of earlier date since the 1565 survey calls it the "olde castell" and describes it as "utterley decayed". A 20m long section of wall of this remains on the north side (where the moat has been filled in), a shorter section on the north and two fragments on the south, the smaller of which has remains of a spiral staircase. A tall tower stood here until it fell in the 1830s. The site is now divided up since the courts now contain separate dwellings, and a stable court fills the north court NE corner.

*Mettingham Castle*

## MILDEN CASTLE    TL 950461

In Stephen's reign the occupant of this motte was said to be a threat to the lands of Bury St Edmunds Abbey around Lidgate Castle. There are traces of a surrounding bailey. The motte has a ditch on the east. Its summit measures 33m by 28m.

## OFFTON CASTLE    TM 065492

The square platform with a wet moat is thought to be the castle held during Stephen's reign by William de Ambli, one of those said to be hostile to the estates of the abbey of Bury St Edmunds.

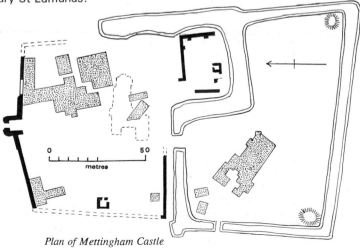

*Plan of Mettingham Castle*

## ORFORD CASTLE    TM 419498    E

Orford is the earliest castle in England for which building accounts survive, these being recorded in the Pipe Rolls of Henry II. It was begun early in 1166 and completed in 1173, the cost being just over £1,400. The work was pushed ahead as fast as possible, two thirds of the money being spent in the two years of construction, probably almost all of it on building the keep, which would have been almost completed before work began on the curtain wall. The second year of expenditure includes payment for stocking it with munitions and 20 marks wages for Bartholomew de Glanville as the first constable. The castle was intended to strengthen the royal position in Suffolk after the castles of Framlingham and Bungay confiscated in 1157 were returned to Hugh Bigod, Earl of Norfolk in 1165. It was completed just in time to play a part in upholding the king's authority during the rebellion of 1173, when it was garrisoned at a cost of £159. The payments noted in the Pipe Rolls include compensation to Ralph le Breton "for his houses which were carried into the castle" presumably to accommodate the extra troops within it. The castle was garrisoned again during the troubles of 1192-3 and in 1215 was held by Hubert de Burgh for King John. In 1217 it was surrendered to Prince Louis of France. During Henry III's reign Roger Bigod had custody of it for a time, whilst at other times the constableship was held by Prince Edward or Philip Marmion. Edward spent £75 on repairing it in 1272-5 and visited the castle as king in 1277, the turrets of the keep being then recovered with lead. Edward put it into a state of defence in 1297, a period when royal relations with the Bigod Earl of Norfolk were strained. Edward II had the castle garrisoned in 1307-8 and in 1317-8 spent £55 on repairs, especially to the well. In 1336 Edward III granted the castle in perpetuity to Robert de Ufford in 1336 and created him Earl of Suffolk the following year. Eventually the building was allowed to decay and in 1930 it was purchased and presented to the Orford Town Trust by Sir Arthur Churchman, and it was handed over to state care in 1962, now being maintained by English Heritage.

*Latrine shutes at Orford*

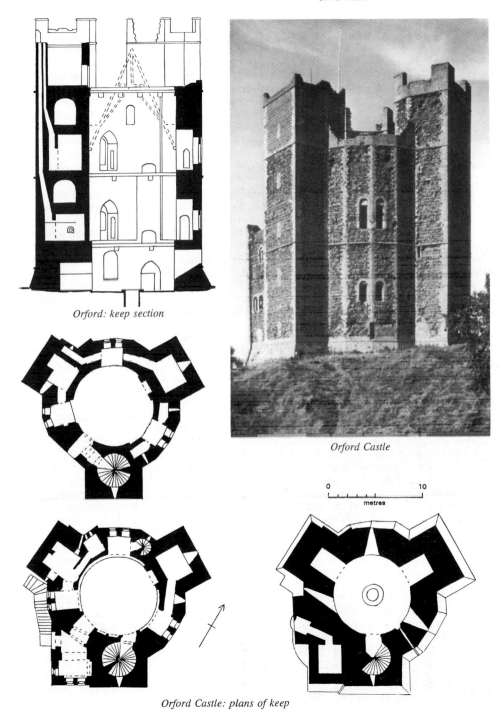

*Orford: keep section*

*Orford Castle*

*Orford Castle: plans of keep*

The castle consisted of a keep enclosed by a curtain wall with several square flanking towers, the same layout as Henry II's later castle at Dover, but on a smaller scale since the court was only about 45m across. The last remaining fragment of the curtain wall, shown on Hooper's engraving of 1785, collapsed in 1841, but a drawing of the castle by John Norden in c1602 shows it when complete. Nothing of it is now visible. The surrounding earthworks have been somewhat disturbed but there seems to have been a surrounding double ditch system and an outer platform to the SW.

The keep is of an advanced experimental design and no other keep in England has a plan-form quite like it. Internally it is circular but externally it is a many-sided polygonal with three regularly spaced rectangular turrets projecting from it, attached to one of which is a forebuilding. Above a broad battered plinth the keep has a diameter of about 14m over walls 3m thick and the turrets are 6m wide. The building is 20m high to the present flat roof in place of the original cone-shaped cap carried on corbels below this level, but rising above it, whilst the turret parapets rise almost another 7m higher. Ashlar is used for the plinth, quoins and dressings but the rest is faced with blocks of local septaria which has not worn so well.

An external flight of steps on the SW side leads up to an entrance vestibule now forming custodian's office and shop. The doorway into the vestibule has a groove for a portcullis which was operated from the almost triangular chapel above. Underneath the vestibule, reached only by a wooden ladder, was a prison with a vent and latrine. A doorway from the vestibule leads into the hall which has a fireplace opposite, a stone bench running round most of the circumference, and three pointed-headed embrasures for windows of two square-headed lights, each light having a round-arched outer order. The east window embrasure has a passage to a chamber in the NE turret. Another chamber above it is reached by a spiral stair from the NW window embrasure, there being the rare feature of a urinal off the passage between stair and chamber. The west turret contains a small kitchen with a fireplace and sink and is reached from the SW window embrasure. From the kitchen (but originally direct from the hall) there is access to a pair of latrines, there being four of these on this side of the building with their shutes side-by-side near ground level. The SE turret next to the forebuilding contains a wide spiral stair leading to upper rooms and battlements and down to the basement, which has three narrow loops (later widened) with their cills steeply rising up in the wall thickness, and pointed-headed recesses in the bases of the other two turrets. There is also a well 10m deep in the centre of the floor.

Corresponding to the upper part of the hall is an intermediate level of rooms in the turrets. The chamber in the NE turret has already been noted. The chamber in the west turret has its own latrine and was probably for the priest since the long passage to it from the main stair leads past the entrance to the chapel. The private chamber on the third storey has three window embrasures like those below and is reached by an L-shaped passage from the main stair, off which passage there is a doorway to the forebuilding roof. From the NW embrasure there is access to a room in the NE turret and to a latrine, whilst there are closets on either side of the east window. The west turret contains a second kitchen reached from the SW embrasure. The topmost chamber in the NE turret can only have been reached by a catwalk around the base of the original conical roof from a doorway of the long passage which connects the main stair to an upper chamber which was perhaps a cistern in the west turret. Chambers in the turrets at parapet level were probably for storing munitions, although that on the NE turret includes an oven.

## OTLEY MOTTE   TM 203546

This is a low ditched motte with a summit 35m across. There are traces of several large outer enclosures of little defensive strength.

*Wingfield Castle*

## WALTON CASTLE

The site of this castle near Felixstowe now lies under the sea. It lay in a corner of a former Roman fort and was captured in 1139 by King Stephen from Hugh Bigod. In 1156 Henry II confiscated the castle and held it until it was dismantled in 1175. In 1173 it withstood a four-day attack by the Earl of Leicester, who had just landed nearby with a force of Flemings. Nothing remains of a pair of artillery forts built by Henry VIII at Langer Point and Langer Rood in the vicinity of Felixstowe.

*Wingfield Castle*

## WINGFIELD CASTLE    TM 222772    V

In 1384 Richard II licensed Michael de la Pole to crenellate his dwellings of Wingfield, Sterfield and Huntingfield. He had married Katherine the daughter and heiress of Sir John Wingfield and in 1385 was created Earl of Suffolk, but his enemies engineered his fall in 1388 and he died in exile the following year. His son, another Michael, who has a lavish monument in the collegiate church, died on campaign with Henry V in 1415 and his grandson was killed just a month later at Agincourt. The latter's brother became Duke of Suffolk in 1448, but was murdered at sea in 1450 whilst attempting to flee into exile. In 1513 Henry VIII executed the last of the line, Edmund, Earl of Suffolk, as a rival claimant to the throne. Much of the building seems to have been dismantled about this time. The timber-framed house of the 1540s on the west side of the court has a porch with worn arms of Sir Henry Jerningham, Master of Hose and Vice-Chamberlain to Henry VIII. The property was sold in 1619 to Thomas Jones and Robert Leman, and it was purchased in 1702 by Sir Charles Turner, although it later returned to the Lemans. In 1779 the castle went to Henry Wilson and in 1886 it was sold to Sir Frederick Adair. The castle was sold yet again a few years ago.

The castle is quadrangular with the north side 82m long, the south side 58m long and the other sides 70m long. It has a wet moat crossed on the south side by a bridge leading to a gatehouse with a pair of three storey semi-polygonal towers. Curtain walls connect the gatehouse to octagonal towers at the SE and SW corners. The work is executed in flint with ashlar corners, openings and framing of the flushwork arcading on the bases of the gatehouse towers. The original two-leaved outer gate with blank tracery survives, set in an arch with a four-centred head. The passage within was intended to be vaulted. Only the base remains of the east and north curtain walls and of the rectangular towers at the NE and NW corners.

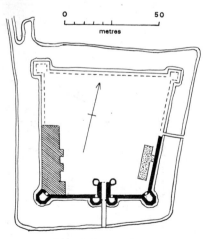

0            50
metres

*Plan of Wingfield Castle*

## OTHER CASTLES IN SUFFOLK

There is a small motte at Redisham (TM 398837) and there is a partial ringwork at Wantisden (TM 354512. There are mounds which may have been used as castles at Chippenham (TL 678670), Finningham (TM 045714), Gipping (081634), Great Finborough (TM 013582), Honington (TL 896742), Norton (TL 950665), Rougham (TL 919642), Sturmer (TL 688443), Sutton (TM 329458) and Whitton (TM 147486).

Moated sites at Nayland (TL 976340) and South Cove (TM 493803) may also have been castles. Claydon Hall (TM 142496) is alleged to be on the site of a castle. There is a reference to a huge wooden tower at Cuckfield in the late 12th century. Richard de Clare, Earl of Gloucester was licensed by Henry III in 1259 to build a castle at Southwold but the outcome of this is unknown.